THE WINES OF THE LOIRE

Regional Guides to the Wines of France

THE WINES OF THE LOIRE

JASPER MORRIS

Series Editor: Simon Loftus

HAMLYN

Half title page picture
Small winemakers tend not to buy new bottles every year but give the old bottles a thorough clean and re-use them.

Title page picture
An idyllic view of the château at Saumur from the banks of the Loire.

First published in 1990
by the Hamlyn Publishing Group Limited
a division of the Octopus Publishing Group
Michelin House
81 Fulham Road
London SW3 6RB

Text © Jasper Morris 1989
Foreword © Simon Loftus 1989
Illustrations © The Hamlyn Publishing Group Limited
1989

ISBN 0 600 56747 8

Produced by Mandarin Offset – printed in Hong Kong

CONTENTS

FOREWORD

The Loire rises within fifty miles of the Rhône, in a region where you can already sense the warmth and smells of the south, but it terminates six hundred miles later at Nantes, in the cold Atlantic.

Its wines reflect the river's changing moods. In the east, in hilly country around the villages of Sancerre and Pouilly-sur-Loire, the water runs fast through narrow banks and the Sauvignon grape makes fresh and springlike wines, sappy and lively. As the river flows west through the water meadows of Touraine, Saumur and Anjou, reflecting the grand châteaux which line its banks, it broadens and drifts at a gentler pace. Chenin Blanc is the dominant grape, producing wines which remind one that this is the Garden of France: they share the succulent character of espalier-trained fruit. Finally, the Loire approaches the Atlantic, passing through a flat landscape swept by a bracing sense of proximity to the bleak ocean. The wines of Muscadet have a crisp edge, an invigorating tartness: ideal for drinking with the local oysters.

Some of the most wonderful wines of France come from the Loire, and some of the worst. They share a common characteristic, high natural acidity, which is the result of growing grapes in a cool climate, close to the limits of viticultural possibility. In good years this acidity enhances the flavours of soft fruit and stimulates the appetite. It's like biting into a fresh-picked peach. When the sun doesn't shine or the grower is too impatient to wait until his grapes are fully ripe you are reminded of the mouth-puckering tartness of green apples.

All too often there is another flavour, most evident when you first sniff the wine, the stink of sulphur. Vital as a preservative (and unnoticeable when used in small quantities) sulphur may be the only means of preventing badly-made wines becoming undrinkable. The combination of excessive sulphur and immature Chenin Blanc is disgusting (but all too typical of mass-produced Vouvray): it is a taste which must have discouraged many enthusiasts from a proper appreciation of the Loire and its vinous treasures. Which is a pity, because there are indeed treasures to be found, sometimes half-concealed by quantities of sub-standard goods, the banal and characterless products of the mass market.

Nowhere are such contrasts more marked than in the classic heartland of Anjou, Saumur and Touraine. This is one of the loveliest wine regions of France, a fertile landscape that is cultivated like a giant garden, dotted with picturesque follies (the châteaux) and centred on a broad river that could hardly have been more pleasing had its course been planned by Le Nôtre or Capability Brown. But just as the vegetables which grow in that most formal of all vegetable gardens, at Villandry, are not really for eating, so (I sometimes feel) with these celebrated wines of the Loire: they are for show, mere decorative mementos of a glorious past. Then I taste a fine bottle of Anjou or Vouvray, from one of the individual growers who still care passionately about what they do, and realize that the past is alive and vigorous in the present.

The best of these wines are wildly unfashionable, sweet and semi-sweet whites which need time to mature in bottle before revealing their full depth of nutty, honeyed flavour. The balancing acidity, which might have seemed unattractive when the wine was young, is now what keeps it fresh and intriguing. Such wines go well with a startling range of food. There's no finer accompaniment to salmon and new potatoes than a mature *demi-sec* Vouvray from one of the handful of outstanding producers. As for the *molleux* wines, they were intended from the beginning of the world to be enjoyed with bread and butter pudding or crème brûlée.

The same variation in quality is true of the reds. Unripe Cabernet Franc must be excellent raw material for wine vinegar; little else. But when the grapes of old vines are picked fully ripe and made carefully into wine by the best growers of Bourgeuil or Chinon you begin to understand what all the fuss is about. Enjoyed cellar-cool, such reds have a rustic elegance which is perfect for rather grand summer drinking and go wonderfully well with poultry. Of course these are not, in general, wines to keep very long but then I doubt if Rabelais (who wrote, fuelled by Chinon) consumed anything that was older than the previous vintage.

The agreeably straightforward character of Muscadet and the rather more sophisticated simplicity of Sancerre find a ready market but the Loire's greatest glories, those unusual reds and classic sweet or *demi-sec* whites languish unloved, save by a few. They do not fit comfortably into standard notions of what is great and they are not made from fashionable grape varieties or matured in new oak casks. This alone would recommend them to the enthusiast, since they enlarge the available range of interesting tastes, but they are also amazing bargains. To the growers this must be disheartening (and means that very few continue to uphold the highest traditions) but it is good news for the wine lover prepared to experiment. Unlike the great names of Bordeaux and Burgundy, the finest wines of the Loire are still affordable: the difficulty is finding them. Here at last is a book to help you in the search, an exhilarating survey of the river's rich diversity of wine.

Nearly a decade ago, I myself decided to write a guide to the wines of the Loire. It was only when I began the research that I realized the scale of what I had so rashly undertaken: the subject is so vast, the problems so general. I seized on the first reasonable excuse (the birth of our daughter) to postpone this enormous project. Jasper Morris has not only relieved me of any necessity to resume work on my abandoned scheme but has made a Herculean task seem like a labour of love.

He writes with authority and tremendous verve, with real understanding and with enthusiasm. His book will immediately become a crib for wine merchants as well as the indispensible guide for consumer and tourist. It is a remarkable achievement.

© Simon Loftus 1989

THE LOIRE VALLEY AND ITS WINES

A vineyard in Bonnezeaux: no great sign of prosperity but the great sweet wines of this appellation are among the grandest in France when they mature.

INTRODUCTION

The grandest river in France runs for nearly 1000 kilometres from its slender source in the Massif Central to its ponderous mouth in the Atlantic beyond Nantes. For half its length the Loire flows northwards, maturing from a stream in the picturesque meadows at the foot of Gerbier de Jonc, through gorges to Le Puy, before descending into the plain. At Orléans the river curves west towards the sea.

By the time it passes Nevers and acquires its first major tributary, the Allier, the Loire reaches senior status. This is the beginning of the Val de Loire, justifiably distinguished as the Garden of France. This pure and perfect region is the home of simple, lasting pleasures. A tourist troubled by the thick accents and obscure dialects of the Midi will be refreshed by the articulate unspoilt French spoken in the Loire valley. The character of the speakers is equally exemplary – avoiding the pompous pride of grander regions or the rustic cunning of more backward spots.

The region's engaging qualities of simplicity and freshness are supported by a classical background. Over many centuries the Val de Loire was a breeding ground for royalty and nobility, who glorified it with magnificent castles built to gratify themselves, their spouses or their mistresses. In the early Middle Ages these castles had a military function too, since Capetian and Valois kings of France could never be certain of the loyalty of their vassals, especially the House of Plantagenet which combined the roles of counts of Anjou, dukes of Aquitaine (from 1152) and kings of England (1154).

Chinon is the grandest of these medieval military castles and the ruins may still be visited. Both Henry II of England, in whose reign the castle was built, and his successor Richard the Lionheart died there. English dominance came to an end shortly afterwards, when Philip Augustus forced King John to renounce his claims, but the threat from England was renewed during the Hundred Years' War. Chinon was the headquarters of Charles VII, whom Joan of Arc aided to revive the French cause through her miraculous vision.

As the age of chivalry and warfare gave way, in the 16th century, to the Renaissance, the Loire valley enjoyed a period of unparalleled brilliance. The château at Amboise was developed by Charles VIII, who subsequently died there from an accident; Francis I, most sumptuous of monarchs, built the magnificent château of Chambord to use as a glorified hunting lodge, while financiers employed their gains to build the dazzling château of Azay-le-Rideau and, most famous of all, Chenonceaux. This grand construction on the River Cher was built in the first quarter of the 16th century and was requisitioned for the use of King Henry II of France's mistress, Diane de Poitiers, who was eventually evicted by her royal rival, Queen Catherine de' Medici.

Other châteaux date from the classical period of the 17th and 18th centuries. Much of Valençay, subsequently the statesman Talleyrand's home, was built at this time.

A happy fortnight could be spent in the Loire valley simply visiting these castles and the other artistic treasures which the region can offer. But what a shame it would be not to take advantage of the food and wine in which the Loire equally excels. At Chenonceaux these pleasures can be combined, since the château has its own vineyard of AC Touraine. (The *appellation contrôlée* system is outlined on page 13).

Certainly eating and drinking impressed François Rabelais, who came from near Chinon, more than the building of castles. Celebrated for his coarseness, this writer nevertheless seems to have had a delicate appreciation of the good things in life. Famous vinous descriptions of his were to refer to wine as 'the good September soup' and to liken Vouvray to taffeta (a sensual stroking of the throat?).

Sadly, the other literary giant of Touraine had less of an appetite for wine than for coffee: Honoré de Balzac, who spent much of his time at Saché, near Azay-le-Rideau, set several volumes of his *Comédie humaine* in the area including, obviously, *Le Curé de Tours*, as well as *Eugénie Grandet*.

Boasting châteaux, literary sources and wine, Touraine is also the focal point for the region's gastronomy. The chef Barrier is once again practising in Tours, where the new star Jean Bardet is now also established. Elsewhere there is a healthy scattering of restaurants graced with single Michelin rosettes but the Loire is not the ideal location for the grandest *haute cuisine*. No gastronomic pomposities here;

GOAT'S CHEESE PIZZA

7 g (¼ oz) fresh yeast
2 tablespoons milk
150 g (¼ lb) strong white flour
1 teaspoon salt
1 egg
2 tablespoons olive oil
goat's cheese, crumbled
fresh herbs, chopped

First prepare the dough for the base. The recipe is based on Elizabeth David's. Firstly cream the fresh yeast with the milk. Sift the flour into a bowl with the salt and warm for 4 or 5 minutes in a low oven (150°C/300°F Gas Mark 2). Add the yeast mixture, then the egg and the olive oil, mix together with your hands. Remove from the bowl and on a floured surface work the dough until smooth. Form into a ball, place in a clean bowl, cover with cling film and leave to rise in a warm place for 1½ to 2 hours.

To make up the pizza; knock down the dough and spread it out to about 6mm (¼ in) thick, either as one large pizza or several smaller ones. Sprinkle with the crumbled goat's cheese and the chopped fresh herbs. Use parsley, thyme, marjoram or oregano and a bit of rosemary or basil.

Bake in a hot oven (230°C/450°F Gas Mark 8) until the dough has risen and the cheese is bubbling and beginning to brown. A delicious variation is to include a layer of thinly sliced tomatoes, marinated in a vinaigrette made with a grainy mustard, under the cheese and herbs, baking as before.

Recipe by ABIGAIL IVERSEN

much better to eat and drink off the land (or the water) and enjoy the pleasures the region has to offer without pretension.

Perhaps, like Patrick de Ladoucette, owner of Château du Nozet in Pouilly Fumé, we might tour the Loire by helicopter. This would enable us to put down at regular intervals to sample the local specialities. We could start on the Atlantic coast with a plateful of oysters (unless, like Brillat-Savarin, you desire them by the hundred), to be washed down with liberal carafes of Muscadet, or Gros Plant for austerer palates. Then upriver to Anjou to enjoy fish, preferably pike, in a *beurre blanc* sauce. One school of cookery writers laments the pitfalls of producing this classic dish; another swears to its simplicity. It is a reduction of white wine, shallots and butter which arrives at a perfect balance of delicacy and piquancy. One of the drier whites of Anjou, perhaps a bottle of Savennières with a little age, would go well here.

A short hop over the border into Touraine provides a meat dish to accompany a bottle of Chinon or Bourgueil – nothing heavy which would clash with the perfumed delicacy of the Cabernet Franc, but something simpler such as a rack of lamb. Pigs are more prolific here than other livestock but the local dish of *rillons* (cooked pork preserved in jars) is not for the faint-stomached.

Fresh fruit, perhaps some of the noted Touraine strawberries, would do nicely to finish our meal, accompanied by a refreshing glass of one of the sweeter Vouvrays or a bottle of the sparkling version. Modernists who prefer their strawberries in red wine should use a Gamay de Touraine. An experimental combination with Cabernet was disgusting!

The last stage of our gastronomic tour takes us to Sancerre for a savoury to finish the meal – or a first course to start the next one! The local goat's cheeses, *crottins*, are excellent to eat at any time: on their own with a bottle of Sancerre, perhaps from the village of Chavignol which is the centre of the goat cheese industry; toasted with a salad and another bottle of Sancerre; or cooked in puff pastry with, of course, the obligatory bottle. Another interesting idea is to introduce the cheese into home-made pizzas, for which a recipe is given above.

The joy of eating and drinking in the Loire is that you can feel bright-eyed and bushy-tailed at the end of the meal as well as beforehand, anticipating the pleasures to come. Neither the food nor any of the wines need lie heavy on the stomach or sharp in the head. There are many other local foods we could have chosen in place of those above – asparagus in Touraine or cherries from Anjou – and the region offers the widest range of wines of any area in France.

THE LOIRE VALLEY

Winemaking came to France with the Romans, spreading up the Rhône valley from Provence to Burgundy and the Loire. If the Romans introduced grapes, it was the Christian church which nurtured them over the following centuries. A number of monks and monasteries appear in the history of wine in every region. The Abbey of Marmoutiers played a major role in encouraging viticulture throughout Touraine, to which region the Abbé Breton, abbot at St-Nicolas-de-Bourgueil, is believed to have introduced the Cabernet Franc grape.

In the later Middle Ages the Loire valley was a focal point for the court and nobility, who doubtless appreciated the local wines. Those of Orléans, which now scarcely exist, were frequently drunk in Paris and Versailles in the 17th and 18th centuries. Paris was ever the arbiter of fashion – more recently the wider fame of Sancerre and Muscadet owes much to their adoption by Parisian café society.

Modern vinous history dates from the second half of the nineteenth century when viticultural disasters reduced the grape from a ubiquitous crop to a more localized phenomenon. First came oidium, a mildew which damaged the vine's health and productivity. Then, more serious still, was the arrival of the beetle *Phylloxera vastatrix* from America. Between 1864 and the 1890s all of France was affected by this bug, which killed vines by attacking their roots. The eventual solution was to plant immune American rootstocks, on to which the local vine varieties could be grafted.

In the short term phylloxera was evidently a disaster, a Malthusian check on the vine population. Thereafter the consequences may be deemed both good and bad: positive, in so far as marginal land was not worth replanting, which reduced the total vineyard area without affecting the quality regions; negative, in that many growers were tempted to re-

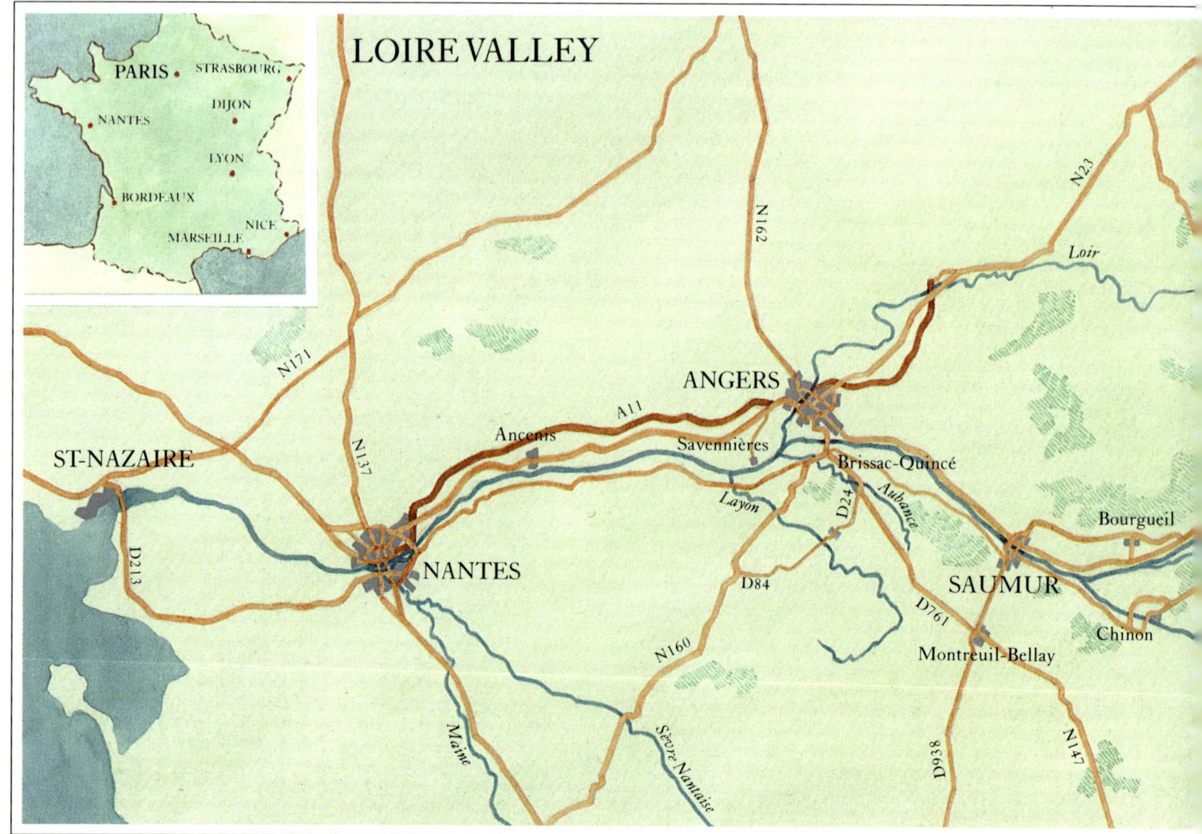

coup their losses by planting high-yielding vines which were not conducive to making quality wines.

By the turn of the century the first moves were being made to regulate production. The principle of guaranteeing certain standards and authenticity for wines from specific areas was first promulgated by the Loi Capus of 1905. From this sprang the *appellation contrôlée* (AC) system now in use. The first appellation to be granted in the Loire, the second in all of France, was Quincy in 1936. Many more followed either side of the Second World War. A subsidiary category, *vins delimités de qualité supérieure* (VDQS), was established in 1973. This covers less famous wines, although the regulations are often as strict as for full AC status. VDQS wines are often from outlying areas like Haut-Poitou and Châteaumeillant, although lesser wines from major districts (Gros Plant du Pays Nantais) also come into this category.

AC first specifies the geographical boundaries of a particular wine: Pouilly Fumé, for example, must come from within seven named communes. Next the rules detail the grape type or types permitted. Some varieties may only be present in small proportions: Bourgueil and Chinon may include up to 10 per cent of Cabernet Sauvignon with the stipulated Cabernet Franc until the year 2000. Some regulations also specify how the vines must be trained and pruned and the density at which they must be planted.

Since quality depends on not producing too much wine, maximum yields are stipulated. These figures are higher than they used to be, a reflection on improved techniques rather than greed, and may be varied according to the circumstances of specific vintages. Large crops are not necessarily less fine than smaller ones, since other criteria are involved, but the *vigneron* who restricts his yield conscientiously should produce consistently better fruit than another who does not prune so severely.

The lowest stipulated maximum yield in the Loire valley is 22 hectolitres per hectare, for Quarts de Chaume. Most of the other appellations for producing sweet or medium sweet wines in Anjou are restricted to 25 hectolitres per hectare, the same yield as for Sauternes in the Bordeaux region. Typical maximum yields for the region's dry white wines are between 45 and 55 hectolitres per hectare, and for red and rosé wines 45 to 50 hectolitres per hectare. The higher figures tend to be at the eastern end of the river. Fifty hectolitres will provide over 6000 bottles after allowing for wastage.

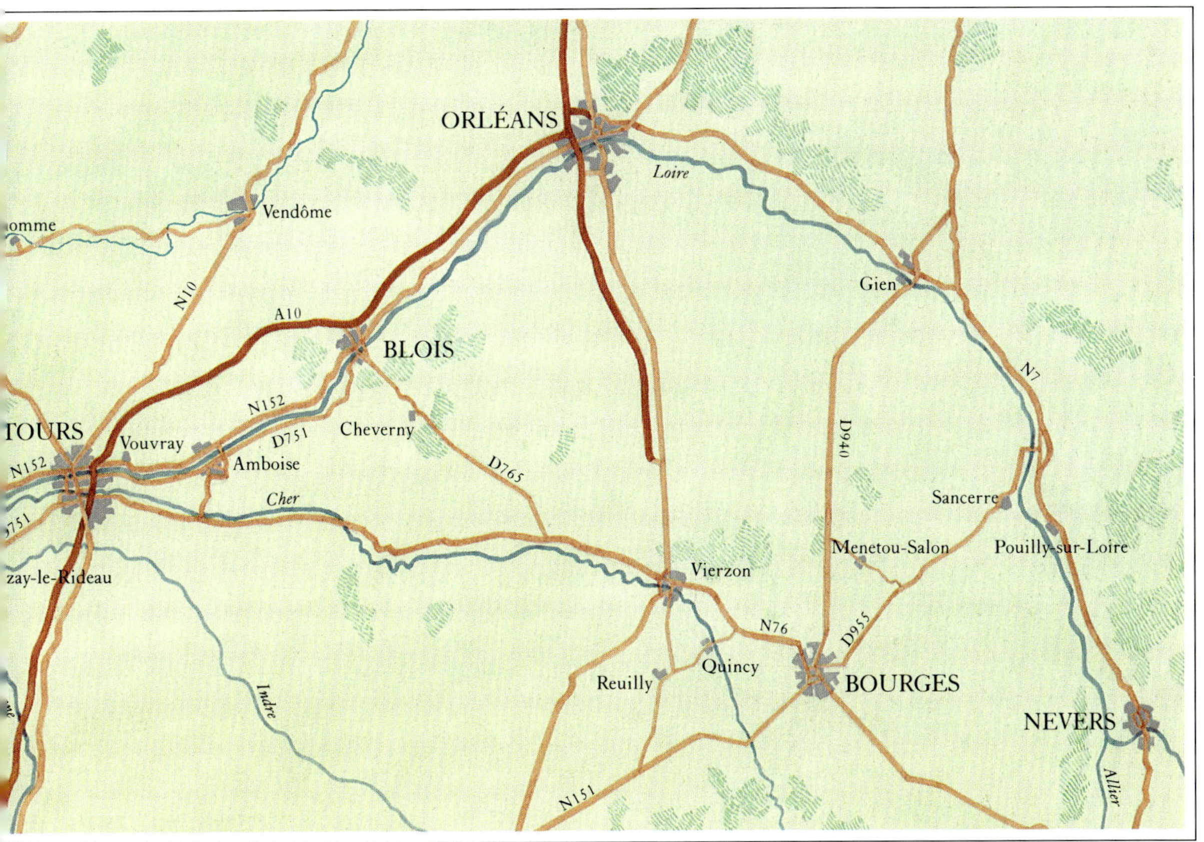

It is also important to guarantee that the grapes are harvested with enough sugar to achieve an acceptable level of alcohol. Accordingly a minimum natural alcoholic degree is stipulated, varying from 8.5° for some sparkling wines, between 9° and 10.5° for the majority of dry still wines and an impressive 13.5° for Bonnezeaux and similar Anjou wines.

Appellation contrôlée status is not an absolute guarantee of quality since the rules allow a fair degree of latitude and policing them is never easy. Nevertheless the system mostly works well. It assists consumers to gauge the style of wine they are about to buy from the label on the bottle, while the emphasis on a specific geographical provenance helps producers in promoting their own areas. Leaving aside cases of deliberate fraud, AC is a fair guarantee of a minimum quality level.

Convention divides the Loire into four viticultural areas running inland from Nantes on a latitude between Chablis and Dijon. The river itself rises far to the south, level with Bordeaux, but there are few vineyards in the uplands of the Massif Central. Two VDQS appellations exist, Côtes du Forez and Côte Roannaise, while the Loire's tributary, the Allier, passes through the Côtes d'Auvergne and St-Pourçain. All these produce rustic wines of local interest, mainly reds from the Gamay grape. The first proper vineyard region begins north of Nevers as the Loire flows between the departments of Cher (left bank) and Nièvre. The latter is really part of greater Burgundy but its principal wine, Pouilly Fumé, clearly belongs to the Loire.

This first region, taking in the Nivernais, the Berry and the Orléanais, has no official designation. Here its various wines have been collected under the heading 'Eastern Loire'; it might equally be called the 'Pays du Sauvignon', for this crisp grape of intense, immediate appeal produces almost all of the area's dry white wines. Pinot Noir contributes most of the modest red and rosé wines which certain appellations also produce.

A combination of motorway and RN 7 puts this part of the Loire in easy reach of Paris and visitors from further afield. The hilltop town of Sancerre is the principal attraction.

The Loire now swings westwards in a wide curve around the marshy no-man's-land of Sologne. This is the country of Alain-Fournier's *Le Grand Meaulnes* and unsuitable for viticulture. From Orléans it is not far to Blois and the heart of the Loire: Touraine.

Plateaux on either side of the river are given over to polyculture – cereals, fruit, vegetables and vines. At first Sauvignon still proliferates along with Gamay but the nearer we approach to Tours the more the classic grapes of the Val de Loire dominate: Chenin Blanc for the whites and Cabernet Franc for the reds. This is also the heart of château country as well as the native region of Rabelais, Balzac and, just a little further south, the philosopher René Descartes.

Touraine offers the widest vinous choice of the four regions: red, white or rosé; still or sparkling; dry, medium or sweet. Vouvray is the most noble of the white wines; Chinon, Bourgueil and St-Nicolas-de-Bourgueil share the honours for the reds. The only drawback to visiting the region is the awkwardness of travel, since the conurbation of Tours separates the above appellations. The vineyards throughout Touraine lie on both sides of the river and bridges are not always conveniently located. The main roads on either bank are often overloaded with traffic – but problems of mobility apart, this is a grand area to visit, rewarding for teetotal tourists, much more so for wine-lovers.

Anjou, including the district of Saumur, also specializes in Chenin Blanc and Cabernet Franc – or Pineau de la Loire and Breton, to use their local names. Life is very much quieter here without the industry of Tours. This is a region of mists and mellow fruitfulness – a combination which provides some of the world's greatest sweet wines in a favourable autumn. A far cry from the much better known Anjou Rosé!

The south bank of the river by Saumur impresses with its collection of ancient limestone caves, a prehistoric housing estate. Some are now used as cellars, others for cultivating mushrooms. After Saumur the cliffs dwindle and limestone gives way to schist. Away from the river the countryside is soft and gentle, a plethora of ruined windmills lending an ageless quality.

The Loire continues to broaden as it approaches Nantes, the final city on the river and, with St-Etienne, the largest. The Pays Nantais savours much more of the Atlantic than the Loire valley. Several grape varieties are grown but this is above all the country of Muscadet, the most heavily planted grape in all the Loire thanks to its concentration here: one gets the impression of an ocean of vines. It is a delightful area to visit, graced by small villages with Breton names, laced with a network of streams feeding the Loire or its tributaries, the Sèvre and the Maine. There are no 'great' wines here but many delightful ones.

The *vignerons* of the Loire are men and women of

The Château du Plessis-Bourré, near Angers, is a typical jewel of the Loire. The reflections in the water make this a gentle pastoral scene despite the imposing fortification.

pride – not a bombastic vanity but a belief in what they do. Every town has its annual wine fair in which producers taste their colleagues' wines and medals are awarded. Yet there is a refreshing lack of cynicism about this operation. Elsewhere the doling-out of medals has fallen into some disrepute but it remains a matter of pride in the Loire, where the leading growers of each appellation are still keen to present their wines and take the honour of a gold medal seriously. In Anjou there is a higher distinction: amongst all the gold-medal winners, one is awarded the Médaille Capus to acknowledge his or her wine as the best and most typical wine of the year.

The producers see themselves very much as natives of Anjou, or Touraine, Pays Nantais or Sancerrois – wherever; much less do they see themselves as belonging to the Val de Loire, a large corporate identity which would help to spread the fame of their wines more widely abroad. Nonetheless it is the Loire which is the connecting thread linking the four main regions and their satellite areas described in this work.

VITICULTURE – GROWING THE GRAPES

Once, before phylloxera, much more of France was covered by vineyards. Nowadays the vine is restricted to areas where its produce can be commercially valuable. This does not necessarily demand the easiest conditions since, for the best results, the vine has to be kept working hard. This far north, between the 47th and 48th parallels, the vine must struggle. Favourable circumstances of microclimate and soil are required and the Loire valley provides them.

The vineyards are rarely far from a river, be it the Loire itself or a tributary: vines are to be found by the banks of the Vienne, Cher, Indre and Loir rivers, the Sèvre and the Maine, the Layon and the Aubance. The larger waterways support the commercial centres. Every stream provides the drainage so vital to a healthy vineyard; the water itself encourages the development of the grapes by reflecting the sun back up through the vines. In certain classic sites autumn heat and humidity play their parts in the development of the 'noble rot' (*pourriture noble* – the fungus mould *Botrytis cinerea*) which creates the great sweet wines of the world.

Controversial though the importance of soil might be to academic oenologists, for those in the vineyards it is a much clearer issue. Soil is very important! Many types are suitable but the resulting wine in each case will be different, year in year out. Soil types may not be able to impart specific flavours to a wine but as for colour, structure and longevity – these aspects can certainly vary.

The underlying rock through most of the Loire valley is limestone, or chalk as it is more familiarly known. It is the subsoil in the Sancerrois, the basis of the riverside cliffs in Anjou and Touraine and remains a feature in the more varied landscape of the Pays Nantais. It makes the greatest impression in areas such as Vouvray or Saumur, where it forms the semi-hard rock known as tufa from which châteaux may be built and cellars may be tunnelled.

The more important role is played by the topsoil, be it clay or gravel, sand, schist or flint. Where Bonnezeaux has a clay and schistous topsoil, Vouvray is chalk and flint. Within Pouilly Fumé the wines may take on different characters, depending on the percentages of chalk, clay and flint in the topsoil. The flintier vineyards appear to give wines of greater depth and longevity. Detailed soil types in this and other vineyard areas are discussed more fully in 'Through the Vineyards'.

Some experts may be able to taste a wine and reflect on the nature of the soil on which it was produced. The impact of the climate, especially the particular weather in a given vintage, can clearly be seen in most wines. But the most significant flavour factor of all must be the grape variety. The Loire valley is rich in this respect: wines of all styles are made from at least a dozen white grape varieties – some of local interest, some world-famous – and nearly as many red. Their character is paramount.

Few of the better-known grape varieties are natives of the Loire. Chenin Blanc, known locally as Pineau de la Loire, is a major exception, being grown in Anjou at least as long ago as the ninth century. No longer the most widely planted *cépage* (grape variety) in the Loire, it remains the stalwart white grape of Anjou-Saumur and source of the greatest wines of Touraine. Chenin has not spread much further afield – except to South Africa where it dominates the white wine scene, California, for neutral cheaper wines, and the cooler climate of New Zealand.

Muscadet is now the most common of the white grapes but although scarcely seen outside the Pays Nantais, it is not a native of the Loire. Sporadic plantings in the 17th century were stepped up after the catastrophic winter of 1709-10. Ink froze in the inkwells at Versailles; the Nantais vines were annihilated, except for a few hardy imports from Burgundy, of a type called Melon de Bourgogne. The survivor flourished and now covers nearly 10,000 hectares in the Pays Nantais, having changed its name to Muscadet, the little musky grape.

Another import to the Loire, this time probably from Bordeaux, is the Sauvignon Blanc; sole incumbent of the white vineyards of the Sancerrois, it is rapidly gaining ground in Touraine and is also to be found in some of the outlying VDQS areas. Locally, and especially at Pouilly, it is referred to as the Blanc Fumé, an alternative name which has spread to the New World. In California, Australia and New Zealand, it may be used to denote a wood-aged wine while Sauvignon Blanc indicates unoaked vinification.

Recently, the other world-wide white wine success story, Chardonnay, has come to the Loire. Here it has no chance to be big-headed, being confined to a small percentage of several lesser appellations – below 20 per cent of Anjou Blanc, for example – or constituting a more significant ingredient in the region's sparkling wines. Chardonnay may also appear in various VDQS wines such as Valençay, St-Pourçain and Haut-Poitou. At Orléans it features as Auvernat Blanc.

Most of the other white grapes also feature as VDQS wines rather than AC, the exception being Chasselas. The single wine made from this grape, Pouilly-sur-Loire, is flattered by its full appellation status. Originally the Chasselas was grown there primarily to supply Paris with table grapes. More important, though only VDQS status, is Gros Plant, known elsewhere as Folle Blanche. Here it is the second grape, in volume and quality, of the Pays Nantais.

Modern straddle tractors are specifically designed for tending vineyards such as these planted with Chenin Blanc in Vouvray.

Chenin Blanc

Chenin Blanc is the native aristocrat of the Loire valley, where it is known as the Pineau de la Loire. Late to flower and ripen, it can still produce the region's finest white wines.

When young, the Chenin's flavours are muted but acidity is the grape's finest characteristic, enabling the wines to last more than half a century. Chenin Blanc produces wines at all levels from workhorse to the finest botrytis-affected sweet wines, as well as a large proportion of the Loire's sparklers.

AC Anjou, Anjou Coteaux de la Loire, Bonnezeaux, Coteaux de l'Aubance, Coteaux du Layon, Coteaux du Loir, Coteaux de Saumur, Jasnières, Montlouis, Quarts de Chaume, Savennières, Saumur.
VDQS Cheverny, Coteaux d'Ancenis, Coteaux du Vendômois, Côtes de Gien, Fiefs Vendéens, Vins du Thouarsais.

Muscadet

The Melon de Bourgogne has fared better in the Loire as Muscadet than it ever did in its native Burgundy. This early-ripening prolific grape makes very acceptable light dry wines in the Pays Nantais, where its resistance to frost has been vital.

In flavour the wines can often be neutral, their particular fruit difficult to specify. Character is introduced by the practice of bottling the better wines after they have been matured on their lees (*sur lie*), imparting a yeasty taste.

Muscadet is normally to be drunk young but it has the capacity to age better than Sauvignon. Muscadet from a good year will take on a richer, creamy character as it ages.

AC Muscadet, Muscadet des Coteaux de la Loire, Muscadet de Sèvre-et-Maine.

Small quantities of various romantic-sounding white grapes also exist – Malvoisie (although it is really Pinot Gris); Romorantin, found in VDQS Cheverny; Tresallier and St-Pierre-Doré which grace the satellite vineyards of St-Pourçain, along with a trace of Aligoté; and Pinot Meunier, here more often called Pinot Menu or Arbois.

Three noble red grapes are found in some quantity: Cabernet Franc, Pinot Noir and Gamay. Cabernet Franc, one of the poor relations in Bordeaux, is the most effective in the Loire, producing the best wines of Touraine and Anjou. It is also becoming more widely planted in the Pays Nantais. The local name is Breton, probably after the Abbé of that name at St-Nicolas-de-Bourgueil in Richelieu's time.

Cabernet Franc's 'elder brother', Cabernet Sauvignon, is rarely found on its own and scarcely grown at all except in Anjou where it is often blended with the Franc. This far north there is insufficient heat to ripen the grape well enough to gain the body and complexity to offset its tannic nature.

In the Loire Gamay never reaches the distinction either of the Cabernet Franc or of Beaujolais, whence the grape has travelled. It provides much of the red gulping wine of Touraine, a certain amount in Anjou and is also planted in the Pays Nantais.

Neither Gamay nor Cabernet is found in the Central Vineyards area (central to France, not the Loire) which is the domain of the Pinot Noir. It would seem bold to plant this far north a variety

SAUVIGNON BLANC

Sauvignon Blanc achieves its highest peak in France (save at a handful of châteaux in Bordeaux) at the eastern end of the Loire valley. It is rapidly spreading in popularity through Touraine, some of the outlying regions and throughout the New World, and is sometimes known as Blanc Fumé.

Sauvignon is an aromatic grape with a piercing, instantly recognizable flavour of gooseberries or blackcurrants. It makes a fresh, crisp wine, stimulating to drink on its own, although suitable to accompany lighter foods. Most Sauvignon wines should be drunk young, within two summers of the vintage, to preserve the fruit.

AC Sancerre, Pouilly Fumé, Ménétou-Salon, Quincy, Reuilly, Sauvignon de Touraine.
VDQS Vins du Haut-Poitou; Côtes de Gien; Châteaumeillant, Cheverny, St-Pourçain; Valençay.

CABERNET FRANC

Poor relation to Cabernet Sauvignon in Bordeaux, Cabernet Franc, or Breton, shows its class in Touraine and Saumur. This far north the ability to flower and ripen early is important.

Cabernet Franc produces wines with a forceful bouquet, part grassy, part summer fruits; they have an intriguing character of great charm but also an austerity which does not please all. Lighter in tannin than Cabernet Sauvignon, these wines show their fruit at an early age but the best wines can last for decades. They soften as they mature without gaining in complexity.

AC Bourgueil, St-Nicolas-de-Bourgueil, Chinon, Saumur-Champigny, Cabernet d'Anjou, Coteaux du Loir, Rosé d'Anjou, Rosé de Loire, Touraine.
VDQS Cheverny, Coteaux d'Ancenis, Coteaux du Vendômois, Valençay, Haut-Poitou, Vins de l'Orléanais, Vins du Thouarsais.

OTHER GRAPE VARIETIES

White grapes	Appellation	Red grapes	Appellation
Chardonnay	Vins de l'Orléanais	Gamay	Touraine
Chasselas	Pouilly-sur-Loire	Pinot Noir	Sancerre, Menetou Salon, Orléanais
Arbois	Cheverny, Valençay	Cot (Malbec)	Touraine
Romorantin	Cheverny	Cabernet Sauvignon	Anjou
Malvoisie	Coteaux d'Ancenis	Groslot	Anjou
Gros Plant	Gros Plant du Pays Nantais	Pineau d'Aunis	Rosé
Tresallier	Saint Pourçain		
Saint-Pierre-Doré	Saint Pourçain		
Aligoté	Saint Pourçain		
Pinot Blanc	Haut Poitou		

Synonyms: Auvernat in the Orléanais refers to Chardonnay (white wines) or Pinot Noir (red). Arbois is the Pinot Meunier or Menu Pineau grape, Malvoisie better known as Pinot Gris, Gros Plant as Folle Blanche and Tresallier as Sacy.

which often struggles to ripen in Burgundy, but respectable wines are made in Sancerre, Menetou-Salon and Reuilly. Small plantings around Gien and Orléans also exist, as well as at Valençay.

The other widespread red grape is Grolleau, or Groslot, a low-quality variety mostly saved for the production of rosé wine. It is high-yielding and devoid of interest, as most bottles of Anjou Rosé demonstrate. The best rosés are made from Cabernet Franc or, in the Eastern Loire, Pinot Noir, although the light pink wine of Reuilly is based on Pinot Gris.

The Year in the Vineyard

Machinery makes the *vigneron*'s life notably less arduous than it used to be. Especially in the large-scale, broader appellations it makes sense to train the vines to facilitate pruning, treating and picking by machine. The more famous vineyards, especially those on steep slopes or where individual selection of bunches is essential, are still harvested by teams of pickers.

The year begins with pruning the vines to remove the dead wood from the previous vintage, leaving a vigorous base for the forthcoming season. Most Loire vines are trained according to the Guyot system, by which the vine is cut back to either a single cane or to two, one each side of the stock. This restricts the number of buds from which the new crop can stem, so keeping yield under control. The regulations for Quincy, for example, allow for either one cane with up to eight buds or two with a maximum of six apiece. More relaxed rules for Muscadet allow for twelve buds on the cane if the Guyot system is to be used rather than a form of bush training.

The first anxious moment for the *vigneron* comes with the rising of the sap in April and budding in May. A frost now would be disastrous, but this is rare in the temperate climate of the Loire valley. Only the eastern end, where the climate is more continental, is dangerously prone to frost. Serious damage befell the vines in Pouilly, where the ground is flatter than in Sancerre, in 1985.

Miniature bunches of grapes form on the vine prior to flowering in late June or early July. A warm, dry spell without much wind is needed. If this passes off well, berries will set and the ripening process begins. The grower now has some idea of the eventual size of the harvest, barring disasters such as hail.

Disease and pests are the main hazards over most of the summer, requiring artificial treatments – although the move towards 'biological' or 'organic' methods, avoiding chemicals, is gathering pace. Madame Joly at Coulée de Serrant, for instance, stresses this aspect of her viticulture. There are tiny insects such as red spider, virus-carrying worms and caterpillars to worry about. The vine may survive these only to fall sick with mildew during a damp period. As the grapes ripen they may be attacked by different forms of rot, or fall prey to birds or passing tourists.

As harvest approaches the grapes turn colour and spraying stops to ensure that the grapes will contain no toxic residue. This is again a critical moment for weather conditions: sunshine is needed to concentrate the sugar in the grape, but not so much heat as to dissipate the balancing acidity.

The Vintage

The date of harvest varies according to the vintage, the grape variety and the temperament of the producer. Obviously, picking cannot begin before the grapes are ripe and that moment will vary from year to year. A precocious vintage in the Loire would start before the end of September, but early to mid-October is more common.

The order of picking depends on the nature of the grape variety. The two major white grapes at opposite ends of the river, Sauvignon and Muscadet, are both quite early ripeners, as is Cabernet Franc. The really backward variety is Chenin Blanc.

Harvesting Chenin Blanc vineyards is likely to take place a good three weeks after Sancerre and it may last much longer. Slow though it may be to ripen, Chenin can produce marvels in a fine *arrière-saison* (late autumn). The sugar content builds up and, in classic years, noble rot affects the grapes, further concentrating both sugar and acidity. In all the main Chenin Blanc appellations, even lowly ones such as Coteaux de Saumur, the regulations require a low yield and high minimum alcohol, and it is stipulated that the pickers must make several passes through the vineyards to select the ripest grapes.

The harvest at Château de Fesles, Bonnezeaux, in 1987 illustrates the risks and possible rewards. A first picking in mid-October produced good results, though not exceptional. Then the rains came. To hold off picking completely would be to risk losing all that was left, so a second helping was taken at the beginning of November, of poorish quality. The weather then cheered up, enabling the formation of some noble rot, and so the final picking (November 15-18) produced some marvellously concentrated grapes of excellent potential.

VINIFICATION – MAKING THE WINE

There is no simple formula for the successful vinification of grape juice into wine. Different styles pose different problems and every wine-maker attempts his own solutions.

Dry White Wines

Most white wines in the Loire are dry and most are for drinking young. Vinification, which means the turning of the grape and its juice into a finished wine, tends to be short, clean and simple – or as simple as this complex operation can be.

The winemaker should have the following basic aims: to convert the sugar in the grape to alcohol through fermentation; to retain the optimum natural flavour in the wine; and to produce a healthy, stable wine without actual or latent faults. Priorities and results vary according to the equipment available, the state of the grapes and whether the producers' ambitions are governed more by profit than by the pursuit of quality.

To outline the processes is not difficult: the grapes have to be pressed to extract their juice. This grape juice, known as the 'must', is then allowed to ferment and the resulting wine is kept in a large container until ready for bottling. The complications stem from the multiple alternatives available to the winemaker at every moment.

The first major step is pressing the white grapes, separated from their stems, to extract the juice. It looks remarkably unattractive at this stage and will need to be allowed to settle for a few hours to let the coarsest deposits precipitate. This can be encouraged

Jean Claude Chatelain is dwarfed by the row of stainless steel vats containing his Pouilly Fumé. This is the ideal material for vinifying Sauvignon based wines.

to happen more quickly by fining or the use of a centrifuge. It is vitally important to have clean, clear juice at this stage.

Recently a refinement has been introduced by many growers, though sharply opposed by others. *Macération pelliculaire* is a system by which the whole grapes are left together in a vat, perhaps for one night, perhaps longer, before pressing so that additional flavour can be extracted. Opponents of this process fear a loss of freshness and that the added aroma and fruit on the palate are short-term phenomena gained at the expense of the wine's balance, so necessary for ageing potential.

To perfect this balance a little human encouragement may be required. If the sun has not produced quite enough natural sugar in the grapes some must be added, a process known as chaptalization. This is frequently necessary in the Loire and is no evil as long as it is used as a corrective measure and not abused – as it would be if very feeble wines were overdosed to give the appearance of normality.

Now the natural yeasts from the vineyard are ready to start converting the must into wine. Some modern producers prefer to clear the must of the natural yeasts and add instead commercial yeast cultures to give them greater control, albeit at the risk of ending up with a more neutral product. The major variables at this point are the type of container to use, the temperature at which the must will ferment and the length of time for the whole process to take place.

For most wines the ideal material for vinification is stainless steel which is inert, easy to manage both for cleanliness and temperature control, but expensive. It is the type of vat which preserves the maximum of freshness and natural aroma in the must, and so is ideal for grape varieties such as Sauvignon. Various other inert materials such as concrete, if lined with epoxy resin, are nearly as effective and will cost less.

The alternative is to put the must into wood casks, usually of oak although chestnut and even ash can be found in the Loire. This changes the wine in two ways: oxygen seeps through the wood, resulting in a slight, controlled oxidation, while the wood itself imparts some flavour to the wine.

The great majority of the light dry white wines of the Loire do not require to be aged or fermented in wood and might well suffer from it. Few regard it as valid for Sauvignon-based wines, although Didier Dagueneau is making exciting experiments to try to prove the opposite, as described later (see page 00). The only white grape variety found along the Loire where the use of barrels can clearly be of positive value is Chenin Blanc. Chenin wines do not rely on primary aromas for their quality but, like those from Chardonnay, they have the capacity to attain the heights of complexity and subtlety of flavour as they age – particularly if they have had the benefit of vinification in oak.

A by-product of the fermentation process is heat, which means that the temperature of the vats needs to be kept under control. It is likely to be higher where wooden barrels are used, since they cannot easily be cooled artificially. Warmth is beneficial for extracting rich fruity aromas from the wine but risky in that the chances of oxidation or bacterial spoilage are greater.

The ideal for most aromatic wines is to ferment at 15 to 18°C (59 to 64°F), which will maintain the crisp fresh quality of the wine without diminishing the power of the fruit. But if cold fermentation is taken too far, the bouquet seems to develop an unnatural character, falsely fruity and unrelated to the grape variety.

Length of fermentation depends on the temperature at which it takes place, since the yeasts work more quickly in the warmth.

In due course the yeasts conclude their work; sugar has become alcohol and the must has been converted to wine. A further fermentation is now possible but this is of another type. The malolactic fermentation needs bacteria (naturally present) rather than yeast to perform. Its function is the conversion of the wine's malic acid (strong and appley) to the softer lactic (milky) variety. This rounds a wine out and removes some of its bite. Although many Loire wines are high in acidity this is such a natural part of their character that producers rarely wish to diminish it, preferring instead to block the malolactic fermentation except maybe in the very meanest of years. Ironically this fermentation happens much more easily with wines already low in acidity than with sharper ones which would benefit.

Once fermentation of both sorts is over, there is little incentive to keep most white wines in their vats much longer. Some producers of Muscadet now like to offer a *vin primeur* (from the recent harvest), after the example of Beaujolais, and this is released in November. Normal bottlings may start in the New Year, gathering pace either side of Easter. Muscadet *sur lie* must be bottled, by law, before 30 June.

The indication *sur lie* denotes a special practice in the vinification of Muscadet introduced to try to impart greater personality to this sometimes dull wine.

This old-fashioned cellar belongs to Pierre Druet in Bourgueil. Last year's red wines are maturing steadily in oak casks typical of Anjou and Touraine.

The name means that the wine is kept on its lees – the deposit formed by the dead yeast cells used up in fermentation – until it is bottled. Dead though they may be, the yeast cells impart some of their flavour to the wine along with some carbon dioxide which has been trapped within them. A slight bubbly prickle characterizes genuine *sur lie* wines.

Medium White Wines

All that distinguishes medium dry (*demi-sec*) wines from their dry counterparts is the presence of residual sugar in the finished wine. (Medium dry is a literal translation from *demi-sec*, but these wines are closer in taste to medium sweet.) A dry wine may have up to four grams of sugar per litre, scarcely detectable. *Demi-sec* wines range from four to 12 grams per litre. Two wines with identical sugar readings may not appear equally sweet, however, as the taste depends on other factors, such as alcohol and acidity, too.

Some wines lend themselves naturally to a *demi-sec* style. Almost all will be from the Chenin Blanc grape, the most famous being Vouvray and Montlouis. Anjou Blanc and, very occasionally, Savennières can also be found as *demi-sec*.

In theory the yeasts will exhaust themselves before all the sugar has been fermented into alcohol but in practice human agency assists. The process of fermentation can be halted either by a dose of sulphur dioxide or by cooling the vats to perhaps 5°C (41°F), at which temperature the yeasts will not function. Subsequent racking and/or filtration will prevent the yeasts returning to their work at a later stage.

Some wines at the cheaper end of the scale are presented as *demi-sec* in a conscious effort to attract that sector of the market which does not like its white wines to be dry. Whatever the quality level involved, it is vital to keep the wine in balance. The higher a wine's acidity, the greater must the residual sugar content be to mask it.

Though the regulations may stipulate what constitutes a *sec* or a *demi-sec* wine, the style is often omitted from the bottle label; this can cause confusion as a seemingly identical wine may actually be dry one year and medium dry the next.

Sweet White Wines

To some degree sweet wines are a continuation of the medium dry principle: the yeasts expire before their work is done, unable to continue once a certain alcohol level has been reached even though sugar remains. Equally, still-functioning yeasts might be deliberately retarded.

The sunniest vineyards of the Coteaux du Layon enjoy this natural sweetness in most years. But more is possible when conditions are perfect. In rare and glorious vintages some grapes are affected by noble rot (see page 16). This significantly increases the potential alcohol of the wine, raising the level of sugar in the grapes to a stage beyond which the yeasts will not function. It may well also be that one aspect of *botrytis*, the noble rot, is to inhibit the action of the yeasts before fermentation is complete. The AC rules for Bonnezeaux require an actual alcoholic minimum of 12 degrees but the potential for 13.5 degrees – i.e. there must be enough residual sugar after fermentation to be capable of producing the extra alcohol if it had been fermented out. In exceptional years the potential alcohol might exceed 20 degrees.

The French word for fine sweet wines is not *doux* but *moelleux*, coming from the word for bone marrow: lubricious and suggestive if not in itself sweet.

Red Wines

Vinifying red grapes is enormously different to making white wines. It is not uncommon for a genius at one to be mediocre at the other. The single biggest difference is in the grape skins. Since the juice from most black grapes is actually white, the must has to be kept in contact with the skins during fermentation in order to extract colour from them.

The traditional method is to take the red grapes, destalk them if the picking machine has not already done so, crush them to free the juice and leave must and skins to ferment together in an open-topped wood or stainless steel vat.

The time spent in the vat, or *cuvaison*, has the dual purpose of macerating the skins in the juice and letting the sugar ferment into alcohol, the latter as with white wines. Cabernet wines in the Loire may spend from eight to ten days in the vats for lesser appellations, and up to 25 days for the superior wines of Chinon and Bourgueil.

Shorter periods of *cuvaison* will not extract enough colour or flavour in this northern climate but modern technology is suggesting one or two alternative stratagems. A system which bubbles nitrogen through closed vats has been tried with success in Anjou and Touraine for Cabernet wines which need to gain suppleness to counteract the grape's natural hard edge.

Another form of vinification known as *macération carbonique* is used for most wines made from Gamay: the grapes are not crushed but are placed whole under a blanket of carbon dioxide gas. The result is the opposite of classical Cabernet – fruity wines with a purple colour and an immediate jammy bouquet.

How to treat the wines thereafter depends on their style and quality level. The simpler reds will be bottled early to preserve their freshness and fruit. The finer wines need time to develop the complexities of which they are capable.

The better red wines are likely to benefit from maturation in wood, though the size and provenance of the barrels will vary according to region, grape variety and producer. There are traditional large *foudres*, often so old and encrusted inside that they are unlikely to affect the wine in any way. In Anjou the *demi-muis* of litres was once common. Then there are the smaller casks, or *fûts*, which vary from a traditional 300-litre capacity to the Burgundian 225-litre (50-gallon) variety.

The age of the cask makes a considerable difference: some producers use new wood which may bring too much aggressive tannin to the wine, though it can equally bring an extra dimension of class if sparingly used. Many growers prefer to buy two- or three-year-old barrels from famous properties in Burgundy (for Sancerre producers) or Bordeaux (Touraine and Anjou).

Rosé Wines

Making pink wines requires no separate skill. The red grapes are picked, destemmed and crushed, as if to make red wine. However, the juice is racked off the skins after 24 hours, by which time it will have taken on the desired hue; this may range from delicate 'partridge eye', to salmon pink, to a light cherry. Thereafter the wine will be vinified as if it were a simple white, never seeing wood and being bottled early to preserve its cheerful freshness.

Sparkling Wines

Sparkling wines may be described as pétillant, crémant or mousseux in ascending order of fizz. Pétillant is what the Germans call *spritzig* – still wine with enough bubbles to tickle the tongue. Crémant is slightly indeterminate; once indicating a sparkling wine at less than full pressure it now has an official standing in the appellation 'Crémant de Loire', described in a later chapter. Mousseux, having mousse, or bubbles, is the real thing. All these categories come loosely under the French title of effervescent wines *vins effervescents*.

The first step in the production of a sparkling wine is the same as for a still one. Standard white wine vinification is used for this – either with white grapes or red ones, the skins being removed instantly after crushing. Regulations permit a higher yield for the grapes and a lower minimum alcohol than for a normal still wine. For example, Vouvray is restricted to 45 hectolitres per hectare and must attain 10.5°; the equivalent figures for Vouvray Mousseux are 55 and 9° respectively.

The bubbles in champagne and other good sparkling wines made by the same method (the term *méthode champenoise* is to be forbidden) come from a second fermentation. The original still wine is dosed with yeasts and sugar so that the natural fermenting process can be repeated artificially. One by-product is the bubbles – actually carbon dioxide; another is dead yeast cells which form a deposit in the bottle.

The final stages are *remuage* and *dégorgement*. The first, which may be carried out either by hand or machine, consists of gradually rotating and upending the bottles so that the sediment slides down to the neck. This deposit is then disgorged (the *dégorgement*) from the top of the bottle without losing any valuable wine.

Since these sparkling wines are aggressively dry and high in acidity they are dosed with a little extra sugar in liquid form at the same time.

Daniel Jarry's exemplary cellars are hewn out of the soft volcanic tufa which typifies Vouvray. Some such cellars stretch for miles beneath the vineyards from which the wine comes.

THE PRODUCERS

Most people discuss wines in terms of appellations ('Let's have some Muscadet for lunch') or vintages ('I had a wonderful '59 the other day'). The style of a wine may be determined by these factors but the quality depends on the skill of the producer. Said producer may be an individual *vigneron* who bottles his own wine, or a major company working on a grand scale. These are the extremes; in between there are all sorts of types of producer. The basic categories are individual grower (*propriétaire*), cooperative (*cave coopérative*) and merchant (*négociant*).

Individual growers are important in the Loire. In many instances the *vigneron* can point to countless generations of ancestors who made wine on the same spot. Sometimes the vine alone may not be an adequate living, especially in the less famed areas such as Coteaux d'Ancenis or Cheverny. These are regions of polyculture where the *vigneron*'s income is supplemented by revenue from other sorts of agriculture – fruits or asparagus perhaps.

In other areas growers can make a healthy living if they have sufficient land under vine. If not, they can always rent vineyards from a retiring grower, or form a sharecropping agreement by which they do the work and take a proportion of the crop as reward.

Our skilful *vigneron* brings the harvest safely in

Scruffily rustic though its external appearance may be, this little cave hides the treasure of Charles Joguet's cellar containing many vintages of his first class Chinon.

but may lack either the talents or the capital to turn the grapes into wine. One alternative is to join a cooperative which will vinify the contributions of its members. In return the grower will receive either payment or the bottled produce.

Cooperatives are particularly useful in areas where prices are low and potential purchasers interested in large volumes. The cooperative bears the financial strain for the producer as well as acting as a corporate marketing body. Economies of scale usually enable a cooperative to offer a competitive tariff.

At either end of the Loire cooperatives are rare, coming more into their own in Anjou and Touraine. Those with a particularly high reputation include St-Cyr-en-Bourg, near Saumur, Confrérie des Vignerons de Oisly et Thesée in the heart of Touraine and La Vallée Coquette for sparkling Vouvray. Another excellent example, from an outlying Loire district, is the Cave Coopérative de Neuville in Haut Poitou.

Alternatively the *vignerons* might prefer to sell their grapes or the unfermented juice after pressing to a *négociant* company. This they can do in a given vintage or every year according to an agreed contract. Another option is to sell the vinified wine to a *négociant* at a later stage to avoid the complications of bottling and selling the produce.

Some *négociants* are local affairs; others cover the full range of Loire wines. Famous in the former category is Ladoucette for Pouilly Fumé. The family now also owns the house of Marc Brédif in Vouvray. Many good red Loire wines come from Couly-Dutheil, who combine their merchant role with significant vineyard holdings in Chinon, and Audebert & Fils who are based in Bourgueil.

Businesses such as La Compagnie de la Vallée de la Loire (Montreuil-Bellay), Les Caves de la Loire (Brissac-Quincé), Rémy Pannier (Saumur) and more recently Guy Saget (Pouilly-sur-Loire) aim to offer the whole range of Loire wines including classic appellations, basic high-volume lines such as Rosé d'Anjou and one or two less usual names from their own area. Their *raison d'être* is to be able to supply vast quantities of wines to clients who need guarantees of continuity and price. Their products are of less interest to the private consumer who is better rewarded looking for more individual wines.

However, in many instances throughout the region our grower will not rely on cooperatives or merchants, but feels competent and is willing to carry through the whole process himself, from growing the grapes to making the wine, bottling and selling it. There is of course no guarantee that the genius in the vines will be equally adept in the cellar; beautifully made wines from perfectly maintained vineyards have been spoiled by careless bottling more than once.

Prosperity surrounds the estate of Gaston Huet, mayor of Vouvray and producer of its finest wines.

Other growers succeed in getting all these aspects right year after year. The best of these achieve a reputation which guarantees the easy sale of each vintage in the fashionable appellations. Some have responded to this by buying in grapes or wine from their neighbours to vinify and bottle as if it were their own produce. Several growers in Pouilly and Sancerre, probably the two easiest appellations in the Loire to sell in the 1980s, have added this miniature *négociant* activity to their own production.

Wine from one of the large band of recognized growers is always likely to be more expensive than from a merchant or cooperative. The justification for this is the greater individual flair to be found in the produce of a good grower: a theory confirmed in practice by high demand.

Château de la Guimonière

COTEAUX DU LAYON CHAUM

APPELLATION COTEAUX DU LAYON CHAUME CONTROLÉE

DOUCET, propriétaire, ROCHEFORT-SUR-LOIRE (Maine-et-Loire)

12,5 % vol.

Product of France Mis en bouteilles au château 75

SUR LIE

PRODUCE OF FRANCE

Clos des Bourguignons

t de Sèvre et Maine

DET DE SÈVRE ET MAINE SUR LIE CONTRÔLÉE

BOUTEILLE AU DOMAINE

ETON, 44190 CLISSON - FRANCE 750ml

Cheverny

APPELLATION D'ORIGINE CHEVERNY

VIN DELIMITÉ DE QUALITÉ SUPERIEURE

Domaine du Salvard

11,8% Vol.

mis en bouteille à la propriété par

G. M. DELAILLE, Viticulteurs 41120 FOUGÈRES

RZ 602

MUSCADET

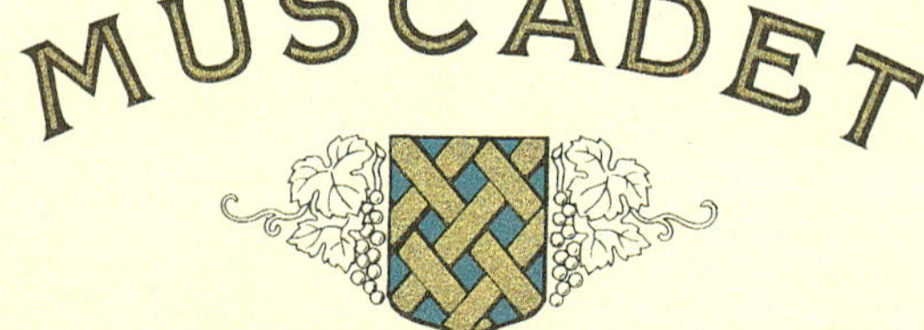

DES COTEAUX DE LA LOIRE

SUR LIE

APPELLATION MUSCADET DES COTEAUX DE LA LOIRE CONTROLÉE

12% vol. MIS EN BOUTEILLE AU DOMAINE PAR e 750 ml

JACQUES GUINDON, SAINT-GÉREON PAR ANCENIS (L.-ATL.) FRANCE

PRODUCE OF FRANCE

A BUYER'S GUIDE

A selection of some of the many labels typical to the Loire valley.

Menetou-Salon
Morogues

APPELLATION MENETOU-SALON MOROGUES CONTROLÉE

75 cl

MIS EN BOUTEILLE A LA PROPRIÉTÉ PAR
Domaine Henry PELLÉ, récoltant à MOROGUES (Cher)
FRANCE

Domaine du Petit Val

BONNEZEAUX

APPELLATION BONNEZEAUX CONTROLEE

13% VOL | MIS EN BOUTEILLES AU DOMAINE | 75 cl

Vincent Goizil .viticulteur .Le Petit Val .Chavagnes 49380

PRODUCT OF FRANCE

POUILLY-FUMÉ

APPELLATION POUILLY-FUMÉ CONTROLÉE

Domaine de Saint-Laurent-l'Abbaye
Mis en bouteille au domaine

e 75 cl | Jean-Claude CHATELAIN | 12,5% vol.

PROPRIÉTAIRE A SAINT-ANDELAIN · POUILLY-S/-LOIRE

WHAT TO LOOK FOR

In any wine region there are producers with widely differing ambitions. At one extreme is the grower who wishes to maximize the profits, regardless of what this means for the quality of the wine as long as it can still be sold; at the other end is the romantic idealist, sometimes heedless of the marketplace in his determination to produce a wine which could not be bettered given the variable circumstances of vine, vineyard and vintage.

Similarly you, the consumer, can decide what to purchase on the basis either of price or of quality. A few minutes' study comparing different price lists will soon show who is offering the cheapest wine of a given appellation. But if that wine has been made without vital love and attention, your money will be wasted. Why waste good money on a bottle which will not give you enjoyment for the sake of saving the few extra pence which a decent bottle might cost?

The question is, how to work out which the good bottles are, for price alone is not a satisfactory guide. There are some excellent inexpensive bottles while some of the pricier offerings may reflect greedy profit margins.

The more work you do, the better your chance of maintaining a high 'strike rate'. The ideal is to go and visit the producers yourself. This is easily done in the Loire valley, a hospitable part of France, where the wine villages are studded with placards advertising local growers. You might visit on the off chance, hoping to find a good supplier, or you might prefer to try specific growers recommended by others. This can be more confusing than it seems at first, as the same names appear on every other house – Bué, in the Sancerre region, has endless different growers from the Roger and Crochet families.

Most growers will be available for visits between 8 a.m. and 12 a.m. and again between 2 p.m. and 6 p.m. from Mondays to Saturdays. They may also receive visitors on Sundays and bank holidays, but usually only by appointment. Few will speak English but happily the French spoken in the Loire valley is the cleanest of the country, practically accentless. This is particularly true towards the eastern end, although rougher elements do start to creep in towards Nantes.

Tastings are free but you will usually be expected to make a purchase if you like the wine.

Visiting the region is not a practical option for the majority. Happily a good range of Loire wines tends to be stocked by all branches of the retail trade: supermarkets, high-street chains and independents. All will carry at least one Muscadet, Sancerre, Pouilly Fumé, a Sauvignon de Touraine or near equivalent, and some representation of Loire reds and rosés. For a wider range ask for the price lists of the handful of merchants who are passionate about the region. They may list anything up to a dozen red Loires, a type of wine traditionally regarded as commercial suicide, and numerous vintages of exciting sweet or semi-sweet Chenin Blanc wines. It should still be possible to buy Vouvray or Bonnezeaux from vintages such as 1947, 1959, 1964 and 1971, though at quite a price – and you may well be unpopular if that is all you wish to buy.

Mostly the Loire provides very good wines for everyday drinking. Hints of greatness are rare, being limited to the grand old whites from Chenin and the occasional, tantalizingly fragrant, exceptional bottle of Cabernet Franc from Chinon or Bourgueil. Very few people think to lay down either sort of wine for their cellar, but they should. It is the only way to guarantee future supplies of mature examples of these exceptional wines.

Those apart, the great majority of Loire wines are for drinking young and thus you can avoid many of the perils inherent in buying good Bordeaux or Burgundy. Young wines ought to be neither ullaged ('ullage' means loss of wine through seepage) nor oxidized. If wines of any colour have a suspiciously brown tint, the symptom of oxidation, they should be rejected.

Wines which are either cloudy or fizzy, or bottles with bits in, should also normally be sent back. There are, however, exceptions. Some growers like to bottle their white wines with a little carbon dioxide to keep the wine fresh, a procedure which imparts a slight prickle or *pétillance* to the wine. This will also be noticeable in Muscadet which has been bottled *sur lie*. A deposit formed in the bottom of a bottle of white wine may seem to be a fault but is not a disaster. It will have been caused by precipitation of tartrate crystals which will not materially affect the taste of

the wine.

Clumsy winemaking can mar a wine without showing up as an immediately identifiable fault. The Loire's particular problem, mostly for cheap wines, is sulphur. It is used as a safeguard against various other faults, as a preventative against oxidation for example, but it is too often seen as a general panacea and applied liberally just in case. Overdosing with it spoils the pleasure in drinking the wine anyway. If the first sniff at the wine reveals no fruit and makes you want to cough, sulphur is the culprit.

As well as genuine faults, rare occurrences, sound wine can sometimes displease because it is not to your taste. One particular factor characterizes almost all Loire wines: high acidity. This keeps them fresh, retains their vital zest, and is an essential part of the wine, so be prepared for it! It is as well to know what you are looking for before you start paying out for the bottles. If you do know what you want, the label on the bottle should tell you if a particular wine is going to fulfil your requirements.

Understanding the Label

The label on a bottle of wine is a guarantee of authenticity, a description of the type of wine it contains and a form of advertising by the producer. It should always be informative, but do not be misled.

The obvious part of the advertising angle is the need to catch the consumer's eye – to make the bottle stand out on a retailer's shelf. Sometimes this is achieved by shock tactics with a brash and gaudy label, sometimes by the classiness of the design. There are subtler, possibly subliminal, aspects to advertising as well. The format, colouring and idiosyncrasies of the label indicate something of the character and philosophy of the producer in question. A chord may be struck between producer and consumer for their mutual benefit.

The label also indicates the sort of producer involved. The words *vigneron* or *viticulteur* or, more commonly, *propriétaire-récoltant* (owner-harvester) indicate that the wine is the produce of an individual grower. The legend *mis(e) en bouteilles a la propriété*

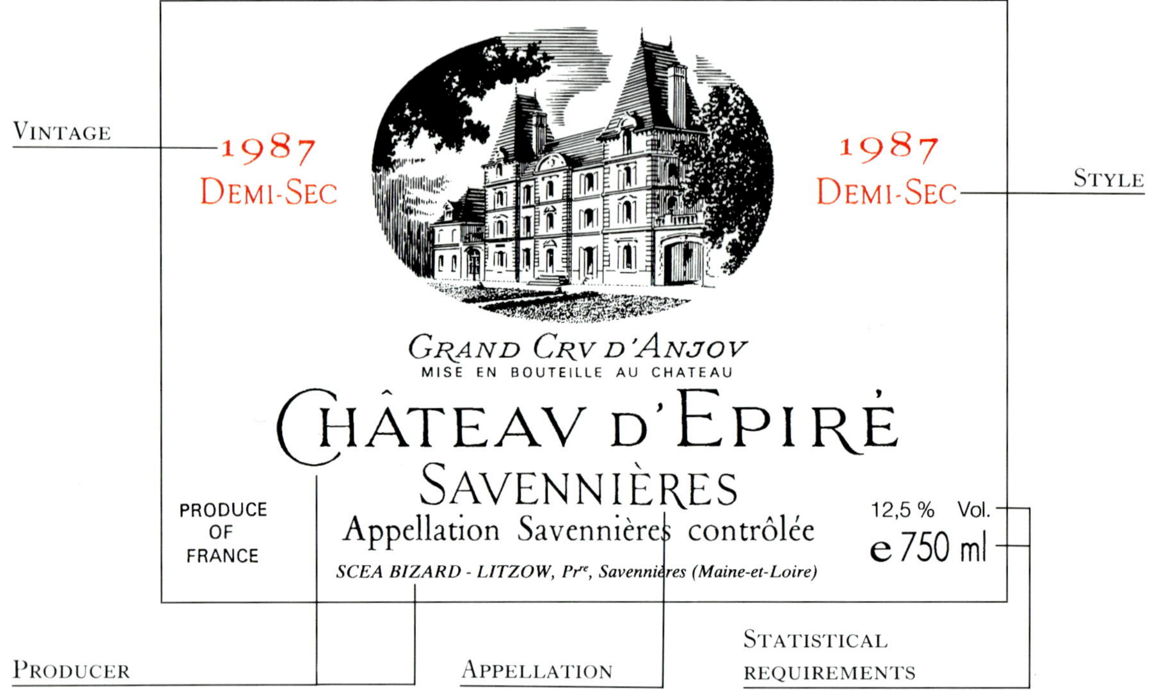

or *au domaine* appears to indicate the same but it is also a format often used by *négociants* to indicate that the wine is from a single provenance rather than one of their general blends. These latter terms are also often used by cooperatives.

The label must identify the wine to certain specifications and may include more detailed information. AC wines, which include the VDQS category, will certainly have the name of the appellation and the vintage, if applicable (see page 33), on the label.

The appellation will certainly specify a geographical location but perhaps only in the broadest form, such as Anjou or Touraine. Sometimes the AC will specify a smaller district (Coteaux du Layon) or a village (Montlouis). In certain instances a particular vineyard may form part of the appellation (Savennières-Coulée de Serrant) but even when this is not the case a vineyard name may often be added (Chinon-Clos de l'Echo).

In some instances, usually for the broader appellations, the grape variety is automatically specified (Anjou Gamay, Gros Plant du Pays Nantais). Where it is not specified it is either because there is a single mandatory grape variety (Sauvignon for Pouilly Fumé) or because the wine is made from a blend, as is often the case for AC Touraine.

Further information, extremely useful but sometimes omitted, defines the style of a wine such as Vouvray: *sec*, *demi-sec* or *moelleux*.

The words *appellation contrôlée*, along with the legend 'produce of France', should guarantee authenticity. Naturally this is not proof against determined fraud but, that excepted, it is a promise of certain standards outlined on page 13.

Other statutory information includes the size of the bottle, usually 37.5, 75, 100 or 150 centilitres. Since May 1988 an indication of alcohol content has also been obligatory, a factor reflecting concern over alcohol abuse. The consumer can now eschew stronger wines in favour of gentler ones such as Muscadet. In practice the cleanliness of a wine is a more significant health factor than its exact alcohol content.

VINTAGES

In some regions the vintage of a wine is a matter of great import and even greater snobbery. In the Loire life is less complicated. The majority of wines, especially dry whites and all rosés, are for early consumption – so one should be happy with the current vintage, shrugging the shoulders if it proves to be a little less fine than its predecessor, beaming all the more in favourable years.

For sparkling wines and the better still whites made from Chenin Blanc the vintage is more important. Producers do not set aside a regular proportion of their crop to be turned into sparkling wine each year but make their decisions according to the style of a vintage. In less ripe years a higher proportion will be ensparkled, since *vin mousseux* can support acidity better than the still version.

Equally, not every year will favour the production of medium sweet wines in the great Chenin Blanc vineyards of Vouvray, and only rare vintages will see the right conditions to make wines in the *moelleux* category.

Knowledge of vintages is also relevant to the better red wines of the Loire. Some will be made in a light, supple style for early drinking in the pattern of the whites and rosés, but the better wines deserve keeping – if the vintage warrants it.

1988 The Loire valley enjoyed its fourth successful vintage in 1988. Most producers consider this year to be finer than 1987.

The dry white wines at both ends of the river are full-bodied and aromatic. Rosé wines and the lighter reds are similarly attractive. In general Loire reds are deeply-coloured and growers in Touraine, who had the patience not to pick too early, have produced some very good wines. Sweet wines are also promising with a certain amount of noble rot which distinguishes a good year.

1987 Conditions were often difficult through the early part of 1987 but, by September, the prognosis was good: perhaps a third success in a row, maybe even an excellent year. Then, in the second week of October, the rain began, dashing hopes of greatness and diluting some wines to mediocrity.

Grapes in the Pays Nantais were mostly picked before the rain, making 1987 a splendid vintage for Muscadet: wines of character which should give a great deal of pleasure. Elsewhere the majority of wines were picked during or after the rain but certain growers who decided to pick early succeeded in making wines of greater depth and concentration than those of their colleagues.

Most Loire wines in 1987 are sound, clean, attractive – but just a little dilute. Many reds lack the colour and concentration of the two previous vintages. Whites from Sancerre and Pouilly are attractive, though lacking the extra depth necessary for the making of prestige *cuvées* (see page 40).

In Touraine the white wines have emerged as *sec* or *demi-sec* in style, soft and suited to early consumption. A higher than usual proportion of the crop was turned into sparkling wine.

Prices remained stable in most areas after the third large crop in a row – total AC production in Touraine was 13 per cent higher than for 1986. Only in the Eastern Loire, where demand has continued to exceed supply, was there a clear price increase.

1986 The Eastern Loire, where the Sauvignon was picked before the end of September in 1986, was the most favoured region. There was enough sun to ripen the grapes perfectly yet the heat was not so aggressive as to scorch them or destroy their acidity. Beautifully balanced, refreshing, crisp and flavour-packed wines were made.

At the other end of the Loire a record crop of Muscadet, 700,000 hectolitres, offered very respectable wines not quite reaching the character and quality of the vintages on either side.

In Touraine and Anjou the sunshine produced deeply coloured but heavily tannic reds, more difficult to assess than the supple wines of 1985. They are less immediately pleasing but there will surely be some fine bottles of 1986 Chinon and Bourgueil for drinking in future years.

The first half of October revelled in a heat wave, perfect weather for the ripening of Chenin Blanc, concentrating both sugar and acidity. Then the weather broke and the grapes were picked without much *pourriture noble*. The high acidity, like the tannin in the reds, means that these wines require long keeping to be seen at their best. It was a good vintage for the production of *demi-sec* wines.

1985 Throughout France 1985 started with disaster and ended in comparative triumph. In January and February temperatures crashed, dropping well below −20° (−4°F) in many parts. The inland climate of Pouilly and Sancerre was the worst affected in the Loire, the flatter vineyards of Pouilly being particularly badly hit. Happily the flowering passed off well and most regions, saving Pouilly, ended up with a large crop.

Once the good weather arrived it remained – so much so that Sauvignon-based wines lack a little of their typical zest, though Muscadet benefited from the sunshine to produce richer, fatter wines than usual. All red wines did well, whether from Pinot Noir, Gamay or Cabernet. The wines are supple, seductively ripe, of good colour and deliciously fruity. The best will keep well, though it is tempting to attack them young.

It was a glorious year for Chenin Blanc. Tasted young, the grand wines of Anjou, such as Bonnezeaux and Savennières, showed a promise unmatched in recent years. First-class wines were produced in Vouvray and Montlouis in all styles – some appealing dry wines which will be drinkable quite young, some more robust *demi-secs* and glorious *moelleux* wines for the long term. There was not very much *pourriture noble* but the balance and ripeness of the grapes was perfect. This could prove to be a vintage in the class of 1959 and 1964.

1984 A mediocre vintage lacking in ripeness nevertheless produced successful wines in the Eastern Loire with typical Sauvignon character. The wines of the Pays Nantais were on the whole mean, the reds throughout the Loire lacking in depth and colour and the Chenin Blancs unexceptional. As always in lesser years the best producers will be able to show some examples which buck the general trend.

1983 This was a year of great promise which may flatter to deceive. Certainly the dry white wines lacked balance, being in many instances too flabby and short on acidity. Powerful Chenin Blancs were made, including numerous *moelleux* wines, but they may prove rather clumsy in comparison to 1985.

The heat also produced a tannic style of red wine, though deceptively fragile in some instances. The best Cabernets will mature successfully over a long period.

1982, 1981 and 1980 A vast crop of sound wines was produced in 1982, but they are too dilute in character and were never suitable for long keeping. The preceding year was more promising, a small and usually overlooked vintage which produced excellent Sauvignons and some attractive Chenin Blanc, but 1980 was mediocre.

The 1970s The only Loire wines still in circulation from the 1970s or earlier will be from Chenin Blanc or the occasional fine Cabernet from 1976 or 1978. Sadly, the unfashionable status of these wines has not encouraged those in the habit of laying down red wines to think of Chinon or its neighbours, so older vintages are hard to come by. The only sources are a producer's cellar or the list of a distinguished restaurant.

Vouvray, Coteaux du Layon and Bonnezeaux from leading vintages may be found a little more easily. Before 1983 the last year capable of producing much in the way of *moelleux* wines was 1976. However, this very hot year ended in drought conditions to which many of the wines bear witness. As well as showing an impressive richness they can often taste rather scorched, which mitigates the pleasure of drinking them.

The real classic of this decade is 1971, a year of great promise which will need a while yet to reach fulfilment. After seventeen years the Vouvray Le Haut-Lieu 1971 from Gaston Huet has only just begun to unfold – enticing nuances of flavour hint at what the wine will produce when it eventually comes to full maturity.

Older Vintages Producers in the Loire are more sparing with their 'vintages of the century' than some other regions. In Vouvray there are two contenders for the title, 1921 and 1947. Wines from either of these years, if no longer youthful, still have a healthy fresh core to them suggesting several more decades of life to come if well stored.

One of these years, 1947, was also quite exceptional for the sweet, white wines of Bonnezeaux: rich in noble rot yet perfectly balanced, and surely amongst the very greatest sweet wines any region has produced.

Other very fine vintages were 1933, 1943, 1945 (although not universally), 1949 (what a decade, the forties!), 1959 and 1964. The last two are only beginning to take on the exciting nuances of great mature sweet wines. The years 1967 and 1969 also had their successes.

PRICE GUIDE

Most Loire wines are produced in sufficiently large quantity to avoid the dramatic price upheavals which affect Chablis. The usual laws of supply and demand apply, dictated by the quantity of a vintage but affected also by quality.

Ideally growers like to take a position once a year when the price for the new vintage will be decided. They take into account the anticipated demand of their customers, the amount of wine they have left in stock, the size of the new vintage, whether its reputation is worth a premium, and how their own running costs have varied according to the state of inflation and taxation. The wines of the Loire are insufficiently famous for a 'charge as much as the traffic can bear' approach.

Take Pouilly Fumé as an example. At the moment, as for several years past, demand is buoyant for this wine. There is nothing left in stock of older vintages, especially after the vineyards here suffered so badly from the great freeze in 1985, and the last few crops have scarcely yielded a full year's supply. Without a vast harvest in 1988, and with capsules and corks, to say nothing of labour, costing more each year, yet another rise seems inevitable. When Pouilly Fumé costs more than Chablis, the bubble ought to burst: so runs the balance of opinion, but as yet there has been no sales resistance to this wine.

If the Sauvignon-based vineyards of the Eastern Loire are enjoying years of fat, life is not so easy further west. Sales are buoyant and prices firm for the more basic appellations of Touraine but the great white wines of Vouvray and the classic reds of Bourgueil and Chinon are selling more slowly. Furthermore there is little premium for the major vintages over the mediocre, so bargains are to be had for those who like these more complicated wines and have the patience to cellar them until maturity.

In Anjou prices are firm for the red wines, reflecting the move away from that erstwhile bulk favourite, Rosé d'Anjou. The Chenin Blanc whites are suffering in the same fashion as Touraine, excepting the most famous appellations. Names such as Bonnezeaux have attracted sufficient public attention to turn the market on its head. Ten years ago young vintages were very cheap and older classics available as relative bargains. Supplies of the latter have dwindled and the new vintages sell at a premium.

Muscadet too has been enjoying a boom, particularly on the export market since vast quantities are being imported into the United Kingdom. The average base price for bulk wine, though nearly double that of Gros Plant, is still very low at just under 6 francs a litre (1986/7) and must surely rise if demand continues at its current high level.

Specifying prices for a given appellation is always difficult because different producers do not charge identical prices. Broadly speaking, examples of a given wine can be bought at two different price levels. One band is for bulk production and will be offered by a cooperative or a *négociant* company, reflecting economies of scale. The other is obtained by the individual domaine.

Prices may not vary greatly within each band. At the bulk level prospective purchasers tend to be very price-conscious so every centime counts. The individual growers, especially if they fix their tariff once a year, will do so in consultation with their neighbours and most will arrive at a similar percentage change. A few growers, by virtue of their reputation, will seek a small premium.

Certain growers in each of the Loire districts have pioneered prestige *cuvées*, limited bottlings of the wine from their best single parcel of vines or a blend of wines coming from their oldest and most favourably placed vines. In some instances the growers are asking half as much again for these *cuvées* above the price of their regular wine but it takes marketing as well as production skills to sell them.

The least expensive wines of the Loire are the Vins de Pays, followed by VDQS wines such as Gros Plant and the generic appellations. Of these Anjou Rosé is usually cheaper than reds or whites such as Gamay or Sauvignon de Touraine.

Basic Muscadet ensures its volume of sales by its cheapness; the Sèvre-et-Maine Sur Lie achieves a worthy premium though still likely to sell for at least £1.00 a bottle less than a young Vouvray or Chinon. Of the young wines for immediate drinking those of the Eastern Loire tend to be the most expensive: Quincy, Reuilly and Menetou-Salon may all exceed £5.00 per bottle, still cheaper than Sancerre and the current favourite, Pouilly Fumé.

CLOS POUSSIE

THROUGH THE VINEYARDS

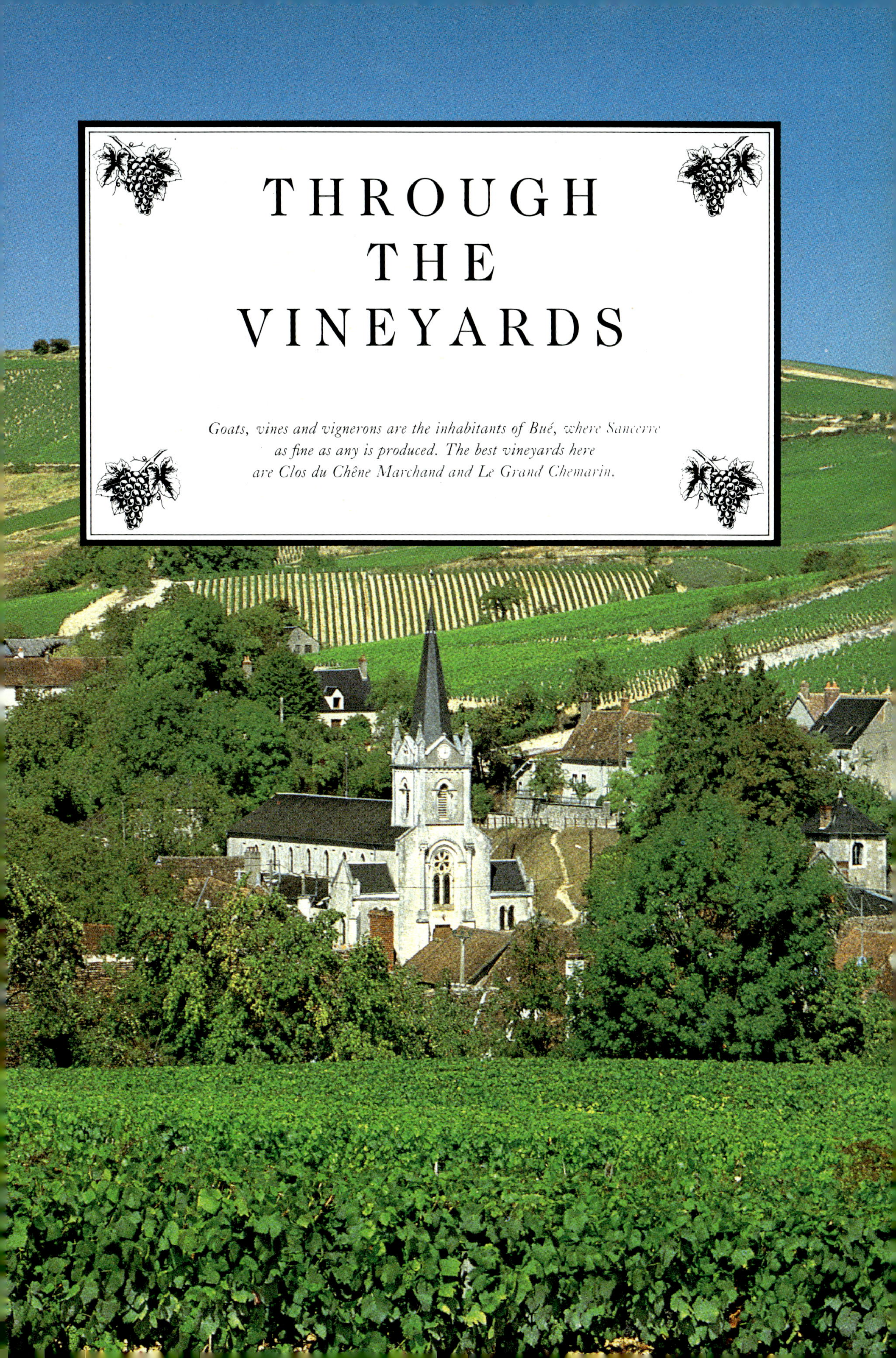

Goats, vines and vignerons are the inhabitants of Bué, where Sancerre as fine as any is produced. The best vineyards here are Clos du Chêne Marchand and Le Grand Chemarin.

The Loire valley being a loose association of several regions rather than a vinous unity, appellations have tended to be local rather than all-embracing. In recent years the establishment of two new appellations and the creation of the Vin de Pays system have introduced the first categories to look beyond individual regions.

In September 1974 the appellation Rosé de Loire was created to cover rosé wines from Anjou, Saumur and Touraine made from the two Cabernets (which must amount to at least 30 per cent of the blend), Pineau d'Aunis, Pinot Noir, Gamay and Groslot. The purpose of this new appellation was to recover some of the ground lost by the falling popularity of slightly sweet Anjou Rosé: Rosé de Loire is obliged to be dry.

The more important of the new creations is Crémant de Loire, introduced in October 1975. This also applies to Anjou, Saumur and Touraine and brings in much stricter rules than previously existed for the sparkling wines of those areas. The yield is restricted to 50 hectolitres per hectare (60 for Touraine) and it is prescribed, as for champagne, that only 100 litres of juice may be pressed from each 150 kilograms of grapes. When bottled, Crémant de Loire must be under at least 3.5 atmospheres pressure.

Crémant de Loire is less fussy about grape varieties than the regional sparkling appellations, and this enables growers to use the increasingly planted Chardonnay. Other grapes allowed are Chenin Blanc, Menu Pineau, both Cabernets, Pinot Noir, Pineau d'Aunis and some Groslot. More and more producers are turning to Crémant de Loire, as opposed to their local sparkling appellation. They are also able to obtain a better price for it.

Chenonceaux, home of the famous royal mistress Diane de Poitiers, is perhaps the most famous château of the Loire. It is also a producer of Touraine wines of reputable quality.

EASTERN LOIRE

A boatman of former times, working downstream from Nevers, would think of himself as passing between the Berry on his left, beneath the citadel of Sancerre, and the Morvan to his right, rolling hills stretching away beyond the port of Pouilly-sur-Loire. Winelovers see the two regions as one, the first major concentration of vineyards on the Loire. This is the country of the Sauvignon Blanc, producer of fine and fruity white wines.

THE APPELLATIONS OF EASTERN LOIRE	
Pouilly Fumé	Reuilly
Pouilly-sur-Loire	Quincy
Sancerre	Coteaux du Giennois VDQS
Menetou-Salon	Vins de l'Orléanais VDQS

Pouilly Fumé

The best wines of Pouilly-sur-Loire are known as Pouilly Fumé or Pouilly Blanc Fumé. Pouilly itself is no longer an entrancing spot. Once a town of some commercial importance, located on both the Loire and the RN 7 from Paris to the south, Pouilly is now bypassed by the main road and has reverted to comparative somnolence.

Vinous activity mostly takes place in hamlets outside the town. Following the narrow road north along the river we pass through Les Loges, home of growers such as Edmond Figeat and Maurice Bailly, to Bois-Gibault and Tracy, at whose château the d'Estutt-Assay family have been making excellent wines for several centuries.

A little further inland are Maltaverne, Bois Fleury, and the hamlet of Les Berthiers where every house has a *vigneron*'s placard – here live three members of the Dagueneau family, Jean-Claude Châtelain and his father, Michel Redde and Gérard Coulbois, all fine producers of Pouilly Fumé. The road through Les Berthiers leads on to St-Andelain.

Between St-Andelain and Pouilly, just visible from the bypass, is the impressive 19th-century Château du Nozet, a fine building but better known as the headquarters of the Ladoucette business, the appellation's most important producers.

Pouilly Fumé must be made entirely from Sauvignon Blanc, or Blanc Fumé as it is often called on this side of the river. The Fumé part of the name refers to the grey smoky bloom which forms on the grapes as they ripen; it is not connected with the smoky bouquet which some tasters find in these wines.

Typical Pouilly Fumé is more grassy than smoky in any case, also recalling blackcurrants, gooseberries, or occasionally a more vegetal flavour such as asparagus. Whatever the exact nuances, all Sauvignon wines should be bursting with fruit, in bouquet and on the palate. Invigorating to drink, the best examples will have enough elegance and persistence to count as wines of real class. But, by and large, they do not gain complexity with age, losing instead the fresh vigour of their fruit.

How widely does Pouilly Fumé differ from its transfluvial neighbour, Sancerre? Some lovers of one claim not to enjoy the other but few could tell them apart in a blind tasting. If there is a difference it is in the slightly greater weight and longevity of some Pouilly Fumés. It is often said that a Sancerre and a Pouilly Fumé from the same producer taste more alike than two wines from the same appellation but different growers. A producer's style of vinification, particularly if the same yeast strains are at work in his cellar, can influence the taste of the wine as much as natural factors such as soil.

In any case, the soil in the Pouilly Fumé appellation is not homogenous. This area forms a gently rolling plateau, without the steeper slopes found in Sancerre. Mostly the soil is a chalky clay, more gravelly in some parts, chalkier in others, especially near Les Loges. One section, the vineyards near St-Andelain, has a significant proportion of flint which provides firmer, longer-lasting wines.

One grower, the bearded eccentric Didier Dagueneau, has decided to exploit the extra potential of this flinty soil. Firstly he picks the grapes later than his neighbours, the better to accentuate the character of the soil; then they are fermented and matured in barrels, very rare now in this region. Furthermore the barrels are new which, by conventional wisdom, should destroy all the fruit in the wine. Dagueneau experiments ceaselessly with different sorts of wood and alternative preparations of the casks, so as to minimize this risk. The finished wine evidently has retained its fruit, clearly has been heavily marked by

Didier Dagueneau's extravagant Pouilly Fumé is in greater demand than the address of his barber!

oak and certainly requires several years to evolve. The future will prove whether or not Didier Dagueneau's enthusiasm is justified, for this is certainly not a conventional Pouilly Fumé.

Textbook wine is produced by Dagueneau's neighbour, Jean-Claude Châtelain, whose techniques emphasize the force of the fruit, giving finesse unencumbered by complexity. Modern stainless steel vats, temperature-controlled, are the principal means of fermentation and storage. Châtelain vinifies the grapes from different parcels separately, so again the differences between chalk, clay and flint can be detected, but he prefers to assemble a homogenous blend so as to provide a consistent product. In the best years he makes a *Cuvée Prestige*, a special selection from the best vats containing the produce of the oldest vines.

This idea was first exploited by the Ladoucette family with their Baron de L, a Pouilly Fumé of grand quality and equivalent price. Baron Patrick de Ladoucette must have a claim to the title of the Loire's most dynamic producer. The sixth of his line, he returned to the family property of Château du Nozet from Argentina after his father's death and took over the business in 1972. Since that time the name of Ladoucette has become, for many people, synonymous with Pouilly Fumé. With the imposing château goes a holding of about 60 hectares, perhaps one-tenth of the Pouilly Fumé appellation. This is vinified at the château along with the grapes and must (increasingly just the former) bought in from local growers, the aggregate accounting for as much as half of the total production of Pouilly Fumé.

The wines are entirely fermented and matured in temperature-controlled stainless steel vats, from which they are bottled according to demand but usually rather later than elsewhere. Most Pouilly is bottled between Easter and later summer; Pouilly Fumé de Ladoucette is more likely to find its way into bottles from the autumn after the vintage through to the following spring. The extra period in vat, safe from risks of oxidation, is thought to concentrate the flavour of the wine.

The finest *cuvées* from successful vintages such as 1985 and 1986 (but not 1984 or 1987) make up the Baron de L, with its special livery and price tag. Can a Sauvignon-based wine be worth that sort of premium? However much purists may doubt it, the response of the market so far has been very favourable.

The Ladoucette empire now spreads beyond Pouilly. They have a successful brand of Sancerre, where they own no vines, under the Comte Lafond label, a flourishing business in Touraine (Baron Briare), and more recently have purchased the business of Marc Brédif in Vouvray. This also is a *négociant* business and, as elsewhere, Baron Patrick will be concentrating on hitting the right formula: stainless steel, consistency of style and attention to quality.

The wine industry in Pouilly thrives. The area having suffered from the freezing conditions of early 1985, when many vines were damaged and some destroyed, there is not enough wine to supply regular customers of this immensely appealing drink. Demand has scarcely been abated by annual price increases.

Pouilly-sur-Loire

Not so happy is the outlook for Pouilly-sur-Loire, a wine produced in the same vineyard area from a different grape, Chasselas. Once planted widely in France, Chasselas is now dwindling rapidly in importance. Before communications were sufficiently improved to open up the vast vineyards of the Midi to Parisians, Pouilly had a thriving trade with the capital in providing table grapes from Chasselas.

Many producers still harvest a Pouilly-sur-Loire along with their Pouilly Fumé, but few with much conviction. For the most part Chasselas produces a dull, insipid wine of no great merit. It has a certain amount of body, no special flavour and oxidizes easily.

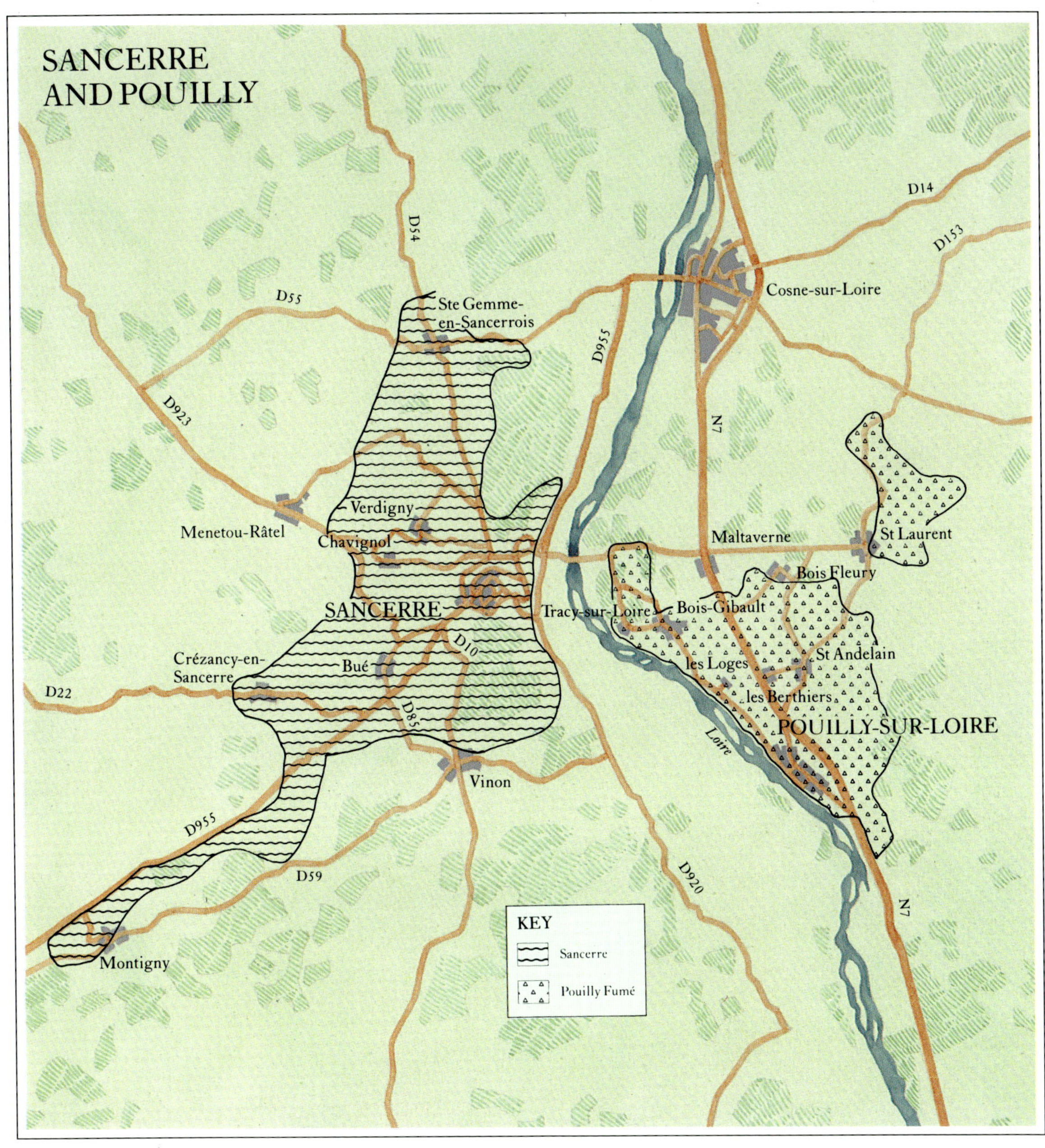

Growers in Pouilly need not mourn the passing of this grape – they will be much better off replanting with the ever-fashionable Sauvignon Blanc.

Sancerre

Sancerre is the town to catch the eye of the tourist. For miles around it stands out as a landmark, perched on its hill. From within the town, the view from the ramparts covers the course of the Loire to the east and the rolling, vine-clad hills of the Sancerrois to the west. The centre of town is attractive too, if overcrowded, with no shortage of cafés and boutiques in which to taste or buy the local specialities of wine and goat's cheese. Amongst numerous places to eat, the Restaurant de la Tour stands out both for its cuisine and wine list.

The flavour of the region is best exemplified by a simple match of food and wine, of a bottle of good Sancerre and a *crottin* of local goat's cheese. Sancerre is a wine for drinking young and fresh, probably in the summer after the vintage, when the Sauvignon's bouquet – of blackcurrants, for example – is at its

Château du Nozet, Pouilly-sur-Loire:
A fairy tale castle with a down to earth approach to wine.
This is the headquarters of Baron Patrick de Ladoucette.

most exquisite. It is not a wine for the grand dinner party at which every guest tries to outdo his neighbour in the refinement of his tasting ability.

Equally the *crottins* should not be regarded as elements of *haute cuisine*. Traditionally, a Sancerrois goatherd would set out for the day with a few hard *crottins* in his pocket to nibble at, paring them intermittently with the specially designed knife which sells so well in the tourist shops. *Crottins*, which take their name from their resemblance to goat's droppings (in shape rather than taste!), can be bought hard and dried, in a firm intermediate version, or fresh, soft and creamy for immediate consumption. Eaten on their own, or toasted on *croûtons* and accompanied with a salad dressed with walnut oil, they are delicious.

The appellation Sancerre covers 14 communes of varying fame. They stretch from Menetou-Râtel and Ste-Gemme to the north, Montigny westwards down the road to Bourges, and Vinon due south. Best-known of the villages are Bué, Chavignol (not itself a commune) and Verdigny.

Bué, the village with the largest area under vine, lies to the west of Sancerre, in a narrow valley of its own. Anybody here not directly involved in the world of wine is certain to be a maker of goat's cheese. Different branches of the Crochet family cover both these industries with great distinction. Other leading growers in the village include Jean-Max Roger, who has branched out by planting vines in Menetou-Salon, and Christian Salmon.

The best individual vineyards are designated by their names on the label. Bué is blessed with several favoured slopes of which Le Chêne Marchand, the slope above the village to the west, is the best known. High-quality wines are also produced from Le Grand Chemarin, and Le Clos du Roy which lies on the border with Crézancy. Paul Millérioux produces a fine example of the latter.

Over the ridge to the north of Bué, Chavignol lies sheltered in its valley below the steep slope of the Côte des Monts Damnés. Chavignol wines have a character of their own, more austere and slower to mature perhaps than Bué. Best-known producer in Chavignol, part-grower and now rapidly expanding *négociant*, is the firm of Henri Bourgeois. As in Bué, there is also a small centre for the production of goat's cheese in Chavignol. Indeed the village is famed for this, as the cheeses go under the official appellation of AC Crottins de Chavignol.

Beyond Chavignol is Verdigny, home of high-class growers such as Bernard Reverdy and the traditionalist Jean Vatan, one of the last to use barrels for his wine, though not new ones. Next to Verdigny comes Sury-en-Vaux, before the vineyards dwindle in importance in the northerly communes.

Sancerre itself is the base of the Vacheron family, producers of sound white Sancerre but more famous for their red wines. This was the speciality of the late Jean Vacheron, the acknowledged genius of Sancerre Rouge. This wine is made from Pinot Noir, a grape difficult enough to succeed with in Burgundy and more fickle still further north in Sancerre. It has also suffered from being the less important wine here, after the Sauvignon. Growers have tended to reserve their most favoured slopes for their white vines, leaving the north-facing parcels for the Pinot Noir, which has naturally been even more reluctant to ripen under these conditions. Not so with Jean Vacheron, who took the Pinot Noir to his heart, planted it on the sunniest slopes and devoted his best attention to its vinification – to the extent of buying second-hand barrels from the famous Domaine de la Romanée Conti in Burgundy. In fine vintages the vines produced sufficiently concentrated fruit to merit such treatment and support the barrel ageing. His Sancerre Rouge had the capacity to improve in bottle and attain a degree of complexity which has eluded most other growers.

Indeed much red Sancerre is a poor thing, insufficiently concentrated to stand up to barrel ageing and perhaps better suited to maturation in ordinary vats to preserve the charming, if uncomplicated, freshness of which such wines are equally capable. Demand remains high and production small, so prices for the red wines often exceed those for the white, which is certainly unjustified on quality grounds.

When red Sancerre was granted its appellation in 1959, so too was the rosé, a wine very much capable of creating a fashion if lacking the stamina to remain a permanent favourite. One school of thought holds this the better usage for the local Pinot Noir, given that the reds can rarely attain serious status. Others believe that Sancerre Rosé falls between two stools, lacking the zest of the white wine without doing justice to the Pinot Noir.

Vinification at least is simple – take the juice away from the red grape skins at an early stage and then treat it as a white wine. Traditionalists may be no more impressed by the colour than by the taste, but the delicate salmon pink of this wine can be very appealing. Being priced on a par with the white wine may remove some of its interest.

Menetou-Salon

Follow the road from Sancerre towards Bourges to find the region's most promising appellation. Granted AC status in 1959 for wines of all three colours, Menetou-Salon is enjoying a resurgence after years of anonymity. Ten communes have the right to this appellation but much the most important is Morogues, whose mayor, Henry Pellé, has been a leading light in establishing Menetou-Salon.

Morogues alone of the 10 communes shares the same soil as Sancerre, Kimmeridgian clay, whereas the remainder of the appellation is on Portlandian soil, a difference which brings to mind the recent controversy in Chablis, involving acrimonious arguments as to whether or not the latter soil enjoyed the same qualities as the former. The consequence here is that the white wines of Morogues are superior to the rest of Menetou-Salon, indeed on a par with Sancerre, while the Pinot Noir flourishes very well throughout. Morogues is further distinguished by being allowed to specify its name on the label.

Menetou-Salon still has land available for planting, so this appellation will expand in future years. Starting from scratch it should be possible to avoid some of the errors of the senior appellation of Sancerre, such as planting Pinot Noir on unfavourable slopes. So far the red wines of Menetou-Salon appear to be at least the equal of, if not superior to, the great majority of Sancerre Rouge.

At the present moment there are only a handful of producers of Menetou-Salon whose wines are seen outside the immediate area. Many of them com-

Morogues, the most important commune of the resurgent appellation of Menetou-Salon has the same soil as Chablis: Kimmeridgian clay on a bed of limestone.

memorate on their labels Jacques Coeur, Minister of Finance to Charles XII and former owner of Menetou-Salon's impressive château. Other leading producers besides Henry Pellé include Pierre Clément at the Domaine de Chatenoy, Alain Gogué, who has recently taken over vinification from his father, and Jacky Rat.

In 1988 the price of Menetou-Salon remains similar to that of Quincy and Reuilly, well below that of Sancerre, though allowance must be made for variations between growers. Henry Pellé reasonably asks as much for his superior single-vineyard Menetou-Salon, Clos des Blanchais, as for his Sancerre. We must expect the price gap between the two appellations to close as more wine is produced in Menetou-Salon, the vines mature and its reputation spreads.

Quincy

Quincy and Reuilly form two enclaves of vineyards well to the west of Sancerre, between Bourges and Vierzon.

For a long time better known than Menetou-Salon – indeed the second appellation ever to be granted in France, after Châteauneuf-du-Pape – Quincy has recently been in the doldrums. The village lies on the River Cher, on a chalk and gravelly soil suitable for the production of white wines from Sauvignon Blanc; this is the sole right of the appellation. The soil mostly derives from the former course of the river, hence the gravel.

The largest producer of Quincy is the Domaine de Maison Blanche, now marketed by the *négociant* Albert Besombes. Amongst the handful of growers

The imposing beauty of the Château at Menetou-Salon is a fine example of the many superb buildings found throughout the Loire valley.

the most highly reputed are Pierre Mardon and Raymond Pipet, who has now retired and been replaced by Denis Jaumier.

Reuilly

The soil of neighbouring Reuilly is chalkier than at Quincy and its white wines from Sauvignon Blanc are mostly unremarkable, lacking the class of a good Sancerre. However the appellation extends to red and rosé wines to be made from Pinot Noir and Pinot Gris. The reds are also unremarkable but Reuilly Rosé has excited more than one expert palate.

The best examples are made from the Pinot Gris, that curious grape formerly known as Tokay in Alsace, occasionally found in Burgundy where it's called Pinot Beurot, prolific in parts of Germany as Rulander and grown at the other end of the Loire by Jacques Guindon in Coteaux d'Ancenis under the name of Malvoisie. All the above are purely white. In Reuilly Pinot Gris, which owes its origin to a corruption of Pinot Noir, produces grapes with a pinkish tinge which make a light rosé of the type classed in France as *vin gris*.

The Cordier family and the recently retired Henri Beurdin are the best-known names of this appellation which is not widely exported. Its cause has not been helped in Anglo-Saxon markets by problems of pronunciation.

Coteaux du Giennois

The remaining vineyards at this end of the Loire are of small repute, producing wines not seen outside the immediate area. One such appellation is the VDQS variously called Côtes de Gien or Coteaux du Giennois, to either of which the name Cosne-sur-Loire may be added. Most of the vineyards nowadays are around Cosne rather than Gien, which is better known for its pottery and a good restaurant with one Michelin star.

White wines may come from Sauvignon Blanc and Chenin Blanc, but in practice come mostly from the former, while reds are divided between Gamay, for the most part, and Pinot Noir.

Vins de l'Orléanais

Orléans is another historic vineyard capital which has died away to the obscurity of VDQS status; it now has only a handful of producers, most of whom require other crops to supplement their income.

A hotch-potch of grape varieties is permitted, though matters are complicated by the usage of local names. Auvernat Rouge turns out to be Pinot Noir, Auvernat Blanc is Chardonnay and the Gris version is Pinot Meunier. These are the basic grape varieties, although Cabernet Franc, here called Noir Dur, is also permitted. Daniel Montigny of Clos de St-Fiacre is the best-known producer.

EASTERN LOIRE – LEADING GROWERS

Appellation	Producer	Village
Sancerre	Lucien Crochet	Bué
	André Dezat	Sury-en-Vaux
	Paul Millérioux	Crézancy
	Bernard Reverdy	Verdigny
	Jean-Max Roger	Bué
	Jean Vacheron	Sancerre
	Jean Vatan	Verdigny
Pouilly Fumé	Maurice Bailly	Les Loges
	Jean-Claude Châtelain	Les Berthiers
	Didier Dagueneau	Les Berthiers
	Edmond Figeat	Les Loges
	De Ladoucette	Château du Nozet
	Domaine de Maltaverne	Maltaverne
	Château de Tracy	Tracy
Menetou-Salon	Pierre Clément	Menetou-Salon
	Henry Pellé	Morogues
	Jacky Rat	Menetou-Salon
	Jean-Max Roger	Bué
Quincy	Denis Jaumier	Quincy
	Pierre Mardon	Quincy
	Raymond Pipet	Quincy
Reuilly	Henri Beurdin	Reuilly
	Cordier Père & Fils	Preuilly

TOURAINE

Touraine is the heart of the Loire for wine-lovers: producing certainly the finest red wines and arguably the finest white wine appellation of the whole valley.

The best of the red vineyards and the best of the white are split by Tours itself, historic university city (twinned with Oxford) and one of the pearls of the Loire. The Abbey of Marmoutiers became the home of St Martin of Tours, who divided his cloak with a beggar.

APPELLATIONS OF TOURAINE	
Touraine	Coteaux du Vendômois VDQS
Touraine-Azay-le-Rideau	Cheverny VDQS
Touraine-Amboise	Valençay VDQS
Touraine-Mesland	Chinon
Vouvray	Bourgueil
Montlouis	St-Nicolas-de-Bourgueil
Jasnières	
Coteaux du Loir	

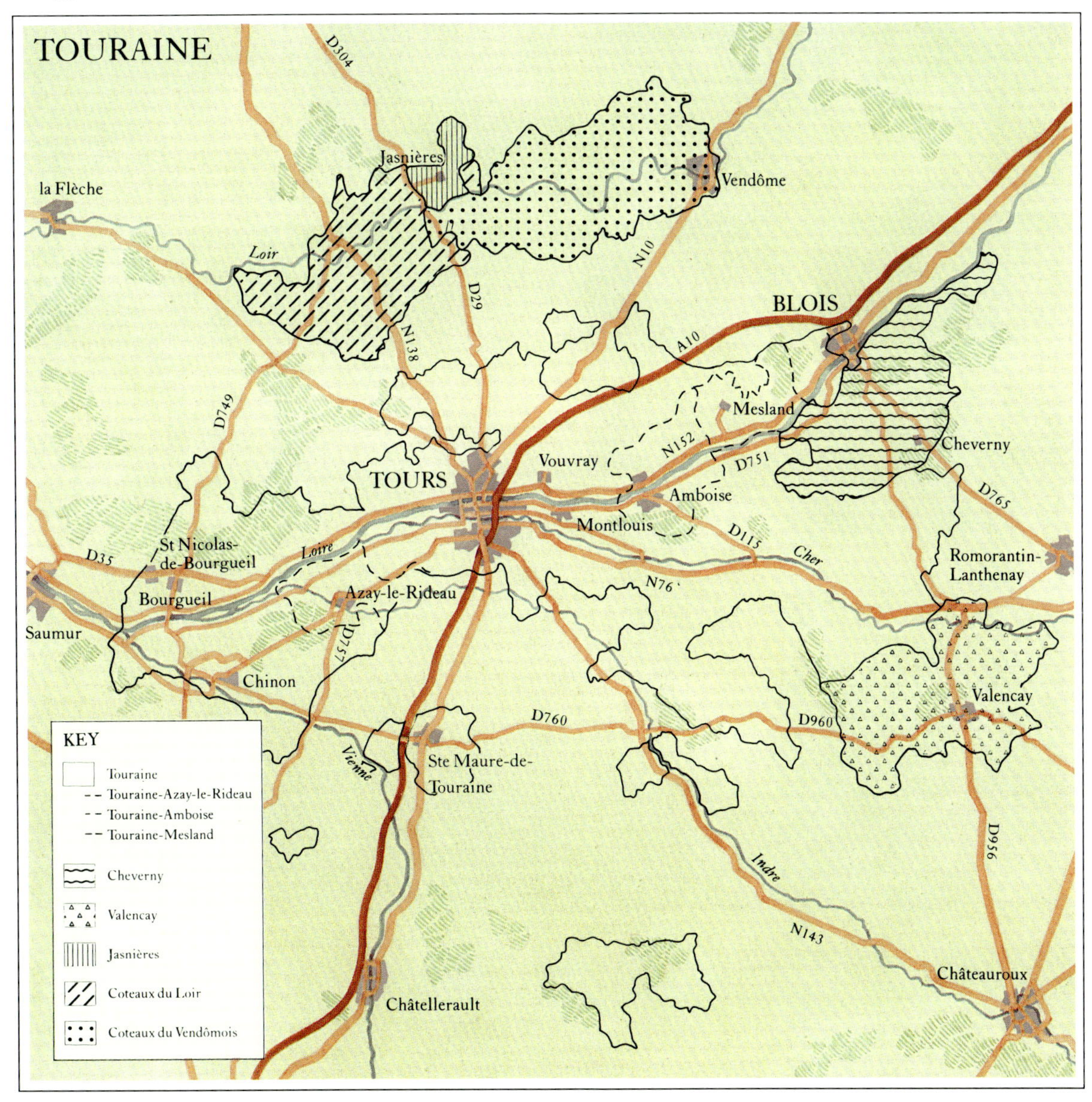

Balzac wrote several of his works at the Château of Azay-le-Rideau which dates from the early sixteenth century. A small amount of good white wine is made under the name Touraine-Azay-le-Rideau.

TOURAINE (GENERIC APPELLATION)

The wide band of vineyards which qualify for AC Touraine lie mostly to the east of Tours. This generic appellation covers over 4500 hectares and includes wine of every style. There is rather more red and rosé than white but the whites are often rather better.

This is an area for the production of delicious fruity light wines, mostly drinkable shortly after bottling and rarely needing to be kept beyond a year or two. The whites are made from Chenin Blanc or Sauvignon – less complex versions of Vouvray and Sancerre, pungent but often rather coarse. Chardonnay may also be included and often is, to ameliorate the assertiveness of the Chenin Blanc. Touraine Sauvignons often take on a smell similar to the asparagus which is so widely grown in neighbouring fields.

Red wines are made from Gamay, Cabernet of both sorts and Cot (Malbec), with Groslot in addition for rosé wines. Gamay is most popular and makes a very cheerful summer drink without the headiness which can mar the pleasure of Beaujolais. The Cabernets are theoretically of greater quality but, as in Anjou, the extraction of adequate colour and fruit in the vinification tends to leave a hard tannic edge which renders them disagreeable in their infancy except to hardened Cabernet-lovers.

Many producers make separate *cuvées* from their red grape varieties, capped by a *cuvée spéciale* which is a blend.

Plentiful though good individual growers are in Touraine, this is not a region which needs to emphasize the 'domaine-bottled' trend. Circumstances of soil, climate and grapes are unable to provide exceptional wines here, no matter how skilled the producer, so the economies of scale which can be practised by cooperatives and good merchants come into their own.

An excellent example is the cooperative Confrérie des Vignerons de Oisly et Thésée. These two villages are not in fact neighbours but the sandier soil of Oisly is excellent Sauvignon territory, while more clay at Thésée forms the basis for successful Gamay wines. Fifty growers who combine over 300 hectares between them benefit from the efficiency of this forward-thinking cooperative. The range of wines is exemplary, each one being clean and characteristic of its variety. As elsewhere, the top-of-the-range white wines are blends of Sauvignon, Chenin and Chardonnay and the reds are Gamay, Cabernet Franc, Cabernet Sauvignon and Cot.

Touraine also has an appellation for its sparkling wine, both white and rosé, though many producers

Charles VIII died here at Amboise in 1498 after bashing his head on his way to watch a game of fives. The wines are rather healthier!

prefer to make Crémant de Loire for which the rules are stricter but the reward is greater. The choice also depends on grape variety – a white Touraine Mousseux must be from Chenin and Arbois, with up to 20 per cent Chardonnay and 30 per cent from various red grapes permissible.

Three sub-divisions within Touraine have their own appellations – Mesland and Amboise to the east of Tours and Azay-le-Rideau to the south-west. Once thriving, the latter is now in a poor condition, as other forms of cultivation have proved more profitable. Only 40 hectares were declared under vine in 1987, much of which belongs to the Château de l'Aulée. Owned by the champagne house Deutz, this property is working hard at restoring some pride to the appellation.

Otherwise prestige has been more or less confined to Gaston Pavy, whose family has been long established at Saché. Even so M. Pavy relies on polyculture for his income. His white wines are made from Chenin Blanc and the rosé from Groslot assisted by a blend of the other Touraine reds. Across the appellation slightly more white than rosé is produced – there is no red.

An hour away by car, if the roads are clear, lies Amboise, whose fine castle is similar in date though in quite a different style to the Renaissance splendour of Azay-le-Rideau. The Amboise appellation lies on both sides of the river, an overflow from the vineyards of Montlouis and Vouvray without quite the same qualities. More red and rosé wines are produced than whites (Chenin Blanc).

Across the river from Amboise and 15 minutes to the east is Mesland, set on a plateau overlooking the north bank of the Loire. This is slightly larger than the other two districts and potentially the finest: indeed the AC regulations require a slightly higher alcoholic minimum here than for Amboise or Azay-le-Rideau.

There being a fair proportion of clay in the soil, red grape varieties are preferred to white in the ratio of five or six to one. Domaine Girault-Artois produces some very successful reds, mixing modern technology with traditional flair, while Domaine Brossillon produces some unusually interesting rosés from Gamay – including a Gamay Moelleux in the warmer years. Permitted grape varieties are the same as for AC Touraine.

Vouvray

Vouvray is perhaps the most noble name of all the appellations of the Loire and yet the wines are so badly understood, so difficult to sell at their true worth. Here the finest Chenin Blanc wines are produced, matchable only by Bonnezeaux, yet in a different style – or styles, for Vouvray can be dry, medium or sweet, still or sparkling.

There are two main problems: too much Vouvray exists in the form of very cheap, mass-produced wine without quality or character; while the plethora of styles available at all levels can confuse the customer, especially when the label is not explicit.

It is easy to disparage the cheaper end of a product range but in this case criticism can be justified. Chenin Blanc is a grape capable of greatness but only under ideal conditions, if slowly nurtured towards fulfilling its potential. All this must be sacrificed when producing wine to meet a low price. The particular culprit is sulphur, needed to stabilize wines in which sugar remains, but a destroyer of bouquet and assailant of the tonsils.

Such are the evils of this form of winemaking that the smell of Chenin Blanc is often described in derogatory terms – dull, flat cardboard – whereas it can produce the most subtly entrancing bouquets of all white wines in the Loire Valley. Sometimes more floral, sometimes more honeyed Chenin Blanc frequently imparts a strong impression of one fruit or another ranging from apples in a raw young wine to a soft scent of pears, while older wines are strongly evocative of quince.

Vouvray has been a favourite for centuries, certainly appreciated by Rabelais. The vineyards lie in eight communes along the north bank of the Loire, starting on the outskirts of Tours. The best-known villages are Vouvray itself and Rochecorbon.

The soil here is part-clay, part-gravel and occasionally flinty, but it is the subsoil which gives Vouvray its special character. The vineyards lie above the villages on a plateau made of tufa, a pliable volcanic limestone. While underground it is comparatively soft and so can easily be dug out – in ancient times to create houses, nowadays for cellars; once exposed to sun and air it toughens up to form a valuable building material, used for the great châteaux of the Loire.

Up above, the vines thrive; down below the bottles mature gracefully, their potential longevity almost always exceeding human patience. Tragically there are but a handful of top-quality producers in this appellation (1799 hectares declared in 1987) and they do not always find their wines easy to sell.

The luck of the vintage is the prime factor in determining the style of a given wine. Vouvray harvests late, well into October and sometimes November, the growers hoping for a warm *arrière-saison*. On the success of the ripening depends the nature of the wine.

The grandest years are those with a fine warm harvest during which some noble rot will have formed on the grapes in the manner of Sauternes. The *vignerons* will then go through their vineyards several times, picking out on each occasion the ripest, rot-affected grapes with which to make the *moelleux* style of Vouvray. For some growers this may only happen one year in 10: he who offers a *moelleux* wine too often should be viewed with suspicion. Perfect ripeness is more the key to this style of wine than the presence of noble rot, very little of which was apparent in the first-rate 1985 vintage when all producers made sweet wines.

Some *moelleux* wines were produced in 1983 and 1976 but the last classic vintage before 1985 was 1971. Seventeen years on, the wines are scarcely mature, still light in colour and needing time to open out. Going further back – as many *vignerons* are able to do, having stocks of older vintages squirrelled away in their limestone tunnels – 1964 and 1959 stand out, then 1947. So far only 1921 can possibly challenge 1947 as the 'vintage of the century'.

There cannot be many vinous treasures to compare with a Vouvray Moelleux 1947. The Foreau family is particularly well off, having several to choose from, since different *cuvées* were bottled separately. Their 'Perruches' was an absolute triumph: still fairly light in colour, a marvellous floral bouquet with all sorts of subtleties, and an astonishing range of flavours in the mouth, finishing youthfully spicy with a long, long aftertaste.

But the great *moelleux* wines are not the only excitement that Vouvray has to offer. Perhaps the most characteristic wines of this fascinating appellation, though again not necessarily possible every year, are the *demi-sec*, medium dry bottles. These may vary in sweetness from the point of view of technical analysis, since years with higher acidity will need more residual sugar to balance it, but the general style should be consistent.

These wines are never flabby, a possible fault often associated by the public with medium dry wines from other regions. The acidity sees to that, giving the wines a fine firm finish. Yet the austerity of this natural acidity which comes with Chenin Blanc is robbed of its offensive edge by the gentle sweetness.

The grapes to make such wines should also have been picked sufficiently ripened to offer an impressive concentration of fruit which should be apparent on the bouquet of even a young wine.

Vouvray Demi-sec can be drunk in many circumstances. Ideal as an aperitif, when the mouth responds well to the touch of sweetness, this style of wine is a marvellous accompaniment to all sorts of food, including those which often seem to be unpartnerable – artichokes, for instance. A classic, mouth watering match is Vouvray and cold, fresh salmon: Vouvray's acidity provides the cutting edge needed by such fatty or oily foods, yet few other wines with any sharpness can also offer enough body to stand up to this type of dish.

Within the category of Vouvray Sec more than one style is possible. Perhaps the wine will be from a meagre year lacking the sun to provide much in the way of a *demi-sec* wine – though if the acidity is too high the wine would be better reserved for conversion to sparkling Vouvray. In pleasant but dilute years a Vouvray Sec is very agreeable to drink young; in rich ripe years a proportion of the crop will still be reserved for the *sec* wines but will be of a suppler style. Indeed some growers specify such wines as *sec tendre*. Yet other vintages may produce hard wines of great potential which need years to mature.

An example of this was a Vouvray Sec 1957, modest vintage, offered by Philippe Foreau. It betrayed its origins by tasting slightly short and flat but the bouquet was first-class: still young and evolving in the glass from one sip to the next, requiring every adjective imaginable for such a wine. The 1986 vintage should also reward patience over 30 years.

A fair proportion of each harvest is reserved for sparkling Vouvray, either genuinely *mousseux* or a lighter *pétillant* wine. After every vintage producers assess the style of the harvest and the state of their stocks before deciding how much should be given bubbles. In 1986 the ration of still wine to sparkling was 60 to 40; the next year, a little less successful, saw just over 50 per cent being declared for sparkling wine. The cooperatives such as that of La Vallée Coquette are excellent sources of Vouvray Mousseux, though every individual grower is sure to produce some of his own. These are certainly the finest sparkling wines of the Loire with genuine character behind the bubbles.

Vouvray needs a brighter image so it is encouraging to note a number of younger *vignerons* responding to the challenge. Frédérick Bourillon Dorléans is one such at Rochecorbon, the Dorléans family

Three generations of the Foreau family.
An aged Vouvray from this estate is as great a wine as one could hope to taste.

having been *vignerons* for six generations. Further up the road, at Parçay-Meslay, is the dynamic Benoit Gautier, while Pascal Delaleu is making exciting wines at the other end of the appellation in the delightfully named Vallée de Cousse.

Yet the younger generation will do well to match the expertise of their elders. Philippe Foreau took over from his father in the early 1980s. Gaston Huet is handing over to his son-in-law, Noël Pinguet. Only in 20 years' time shall we really see if the successors to the legendary names, or their young competitors, can produce wines of equal greatness.

For the time being the wines of Foreau and Huet act as benchmarks. Foreau wines tend to be full and ripe, when the year and style allow, yet with a noticeable acidity to confirm their potential longevity. This acidity is better masked chez Huet, the mayor of Vouvray. His wines have a firm structure which keeps each of the component elements, fruit and austerity, elegance and concentration, in its place until maturity draws out all their nuances. Closed though they may seem when young, these wines are clearly of the highest class.

Vouvray needs to match youthful vigour with the experience and traditional expertise of the older generation in order to rediscover the original fame of this marvellous wine. The signs are propitous. It will be particularly interesting to see how the new broom of the Ladoucette organization revives another famous name of Vouvray, Marc Bredif.

Montlouis

The small town of Montlouis, across the river from Vouvray, is usually considered as a poor man's version of the more famous wine. This is unfair although this opinion does contain a kernel of truth: the wines are similar in style to Vouvray but cheaper.

Nevertheless Montlouis has remained very much in Vouvray's shadow, perhaps because the more important road runs along the north bank of the river. Montlouis has always been less fashionable, as the lack of sophistication of most labels indicates. Originally the *vignerons* of Montlouis expected to be included in the Vouvray appellation but were rejected so formed their own. If the wines do differ from Vouvray it is because the soil is rather sandier, giving wines that are a touch lighter, not always quite so acidic, and maybe not able to age as long.

Montlouis wines can be produced in three communes – Montlouis itself, St-Martin-le-Beau and, less importantly, Lussault. Most of the better-known growers are to be found in St-Martin.

The most distinguished growers are the brothers Berger of the Domaine des Liards, whose prime vineyards seem to produce a more opulent style of Montlouis than the average. The Bergers also specialize in producing sparkling wines both from their own grapes and on behalf of others.

Another excellent producer at St-Martin-le-Beau is Gilles Verley, a relative newcomer to the region. At a blind tasting of Montlouis wines in London his stood out consistently for their clean, fresh style, beautifully constructed and full of fruit.

Better known and equally impressive are Dominique Moyer in Montlouis and G. Délétang, who also produces an excellent Sauvignon de Touraine, at St-Martin. Montlouis also has a cooperative, a source of sound inexpensive wine.

Montlouis suffers from its position in the shade but the consumer can profit from it. The price differential between fine and mediocre vintages is insufficient, so stock up with wines, perhaps from several different sources, in the successful years.

Jasnières

This little appellation is not as forgotten as one might expect. The hamlet which gives it its name is tiny, consisting of a farmhouse or two a few minutes away from the small town of Lhomme. Here we are well to the north of Tours, not on the banks of *la* Loire but of its tributary, *le* Loir.

Nevertheless this is classic Chenin Blanc country, boasting a subsoil of tufa similar to Vouvray's and equally suitable for the hollowing-out of cellars. Jasnières was once well known, mentioned in the 19th century and an early qualifier for appellation status in 1937. Since then production has dwindled, though there seems no immediate risk of extinction. Two growers, Joël Gigou and Jean-Baptiste Pinon, are currently the most prominent flag-bearers.

Jasnières is always white, always Chenin Blanc. This far north the wines are usually produced in the dry style, requiring patience to allow them to mellow. Distinguished by elegance, they are equally marked by their austerity.

Coteaux du Loir

Also based on the town of Lhomme, the appellation Coteaux du Loir covers more ground – though not much more is planted – and more styles of wine than Jasnières. White wines must still be from the Chenin Blanc but AC regulations allow red wines from Pineau d'Aunis, Cabernet, Gamay and Cot, to which 25 per cent of Groslot may be added for the rosé.

Coteaux du Vendômois

Moving east from Lhomme, towards Vendôme, we find the VDQS area of Coteaux du Vendômois, spanning both sides of the River Loir. White wines must be made from Chenin Blanc, with a little Chardonnay permitted, rosé wines from Pineau d'Aunis (plus Gamay up to 30 per cent) and the reds from at least 30 per cent Pineau d'Aunis to which may be added Gamay, Pinot Noir or Cabernet.

Very little wine is produced.

Cheverny

More famous for its château than its wines, Cheverny has some interesting and unusual bottles to offer. This VDQS comprises quite a hotch-potch of different grape types, making wines of all three colours.

Red wines are most likely to be light gulpable Gamays, but Cabernet Franc, Cabernet Sauvignon, Cot (or Malbec) and Pinot Noir are all permitted and exist in blends or as varietal wines. These grapes may equally produce rosés, for which Pineau d'Aunis and Pinot Gris are also allowed.

Cheverny is better known for its light, dry and sometimes too acidic white wines. Amongst the principal white grapes are the Loire favourites, Chenin Blanc and Sauvignon, while Arbois and Chardonnay are also found. The region's speciality is Romorantin, a grape unique to this appellation and presumably deriving its name from the neighbouring town.

Best-known growers of Cheverny are the Domaine du Salvard, run by the Delaille family, and the Domaine Gendrier, but most wine is produced by cooperatives.

Valençay

Valençay has a VDQS appellation in the south-east corner of Touraine; like Cheverny, it is better known for its château, and rightly so. Red wines can be made from Cabernet Franc, Cabernet Sauvignon, Cot, Pinot Noir and Gamay, with up to 25 per cent of various lesser-quality varieties. Whites are from Chardonnay, Arbois or Sauvignon; surprisingly Chenin Blanc, along with the rare Romorantin, is relegated to being a minority component, maximum 40 per cent.

Production is small and Valençay wines are rarely to be found outside their district.

Chinon

Chinon's most famous literary son is François Rabelais, a fact celebrated unremittingly in the names of streets, restaurants and hotels. His bulbous leering face appears on a fair number of wine labels as well, often accompanied by a bibulous motto from his works such as *'beuvez tousjours ne mourrez jamais'*. There are rewards for the daily consumption of good wine but as yet immortality is not one of them.

Chinon is capital of Cabernet Franc country. It is the best known of the trio of appellations in Touraine specializing in this grape variety. With 1545 hectares under vine it is also the biggest, covering 19 communes on the banks of the Loire and Vienne rivers. Some of the vineyards are close to Chinon itself; others adorn the flatter ground near Beaumont-en-Véron. The third well-known site is on the north bank of the Vienne at Cravant-les-Coteaux.

Some Chinon wines are soft and supple for early drinking; others can mature gracefully for decades, as the wine list at 'Au Plaisir Gourmand' bears out. Much depends on where the wine was produced and on which of three basic soil types it was grown.

The light, fresh style for early consumption comes from the mainly sandy soil in the valley of the Vienne – although the AC regulations expressly rule out soil comprising recent alluvial deposits (*alluvions modernes*) since it is too rich for the production of decent wine.

More robust wines, capable of developing greater complexity in bottle, are grown on chalk, clay and gravelly slopes, such as those found at Cravant.

Above Chinon and between the two rivers the ground forms a chalk-based plateau on which deep-coloured, long-lived Chinons can be made. Part of the plateau is covered by the forest of Chinon and is excluded from the appellation, but vineyards on the remainder are much sought after.

The starting point for a first-time visitor to the appellation should be the Maison Couly-Dutheil, distinguished growers and capable merchants, in Chinon itself. As *négociants* they supervise a fair proportion of the wines of Chinon, maturing them in their impressive 12th-century chalk caves. However, the feathers in their cap are some prime vineyards at the top of the hill above Chinon, which include the celebrated Clos de l'Echo.

One road out of Chinon leads eastwards along the north bank of the Vienne to Cravant-les-Coteaux where nearly half of all Chinon is produced. Several of the region's better growers can be found here, including the brothers Jean and Bernard Baudry who each run domaines. Bernard Baudry is a believer in the use of new oak, if kept in proportion, to add greater elegance to the wine.

Chinon is famous for its castle, where Joan of Arc first approached the Dauphin, Rabelais who was born near here and its excellent red wines made from Cabernet Franc.

Across the river from Cravant is Sazilly which may be revered by future generations as the home of Charles Joguet, talented sculptor and exceptional *vigneron*, a man with an unsurpassed understanding of wine. His latest experiment, in league with the region's gifted oenologist Jacques Puisais, is the planting of a parcel of selected ungrafted vines with a view to finding out what the pre-phylloxera article must have been like. Joguet is one of the truly serious *vignerons* who vinifies, then matures and bottles his various wines from different locations separately, each one preserving its special characteristics whatever the vintage.

Another road runs west from Chinon before turning north towards the Loire via the villages of Beaumont and Savigny-en-Véron. For once the scenery is comparatively dismal but there are vinous rewards, especially those provided by one branch or another of the extensive Raffault family. Domaine Olga Raffault also produces that rarity, a white Chinon made from Chenin Blanc.

Bourgueil

Source of wonderful red wines, Bourgueil lacks some of Chinon's natural assets: the name is more difficult to spell and pronounce, especially for foreigners, and Rabelais was not brought up there. It is also a smaller town without the commercial and tourist advantages which Chinon enjoys.

Yet just possibly the finest red Loire wines of all come from Bourgueil. A comparison between the wines of Bourgueil and Chinon is very hard unless in the cellar of a *vigneron* who has both appellations. Then the Chinon shows itself to be a solid chunky wine, maybe a little unwieldy; by contrast the best of Bourgueil has a graceful dimension to soften the rough edges of the Cabernet Franc which, as in Chinon, must be the grape variety.

Much depends on the soil which, also as in Chinon, varies across the appellation between sandy, gravelly and tufa. Bourgueil is produced in eight communes including the hamlets of Restigné, Ingrandes-de-Touraine and Benais.

Paul Maître and Pierre-Jacques Druet have both made their home in Benais. Druet is one of those impassioned winemakers who seems crazy to his colleagues. A native of the Loire but owning no vines himself, he learned his trade in vineyards throughout France before choosing to settle in Benais. Here he has been able to rent some ideal vineyards – old vines in excellent locations – from which he makes some of the finest red wines of the Loire.

As with his friend Charles Joguet in Chinon, Druet's cellars are spread across numerous locations. One houses the stainless steel vinification vats (Druet has had them specially made to imitate the sloping shape of the old wooden ones), another his stock of bottles. A third, a cave dug out from the limestone beneath his vines, is for maturing the wine in barrels. Bourgueil in the hands of a master such as Druet becomes a serious red wine – deep in colour, powerful without being overblown, full of fruit yet with an enticing spicy edge.

Each of the Druet wines is a perfect reflection of the soil from which it originates. One *cuvée* is soft, supple, for drinking very young. Another is firmer, longer-lasting, with a greater degree of concentration. Finally there is the Cuvée Grands Monts, grown on tufa, which is the real *vin de garde*, unapproachable for five years and deserving much longer.

Other good producers of Bourgueil, on a larger scale, are the Lamé-Delille-Boucard family at Ingrandes and Audebert & Fils in Bourgueil itself. The former offers several different *cuvées* and still has stocks of older vintages which prove that even the lighter style of Bourgueil can age agreeably. Audebert & Fils owns vineyards but is better known in its *négociant* capacity, a specialist in Loire reds and particularly strong in sales to restaurants.

St-Nicolas de Bourgueil

The commune of St-Nicolas is included in the eight which make up Bourgueil but has the right to use its own name. Annual production is about two-thirds that of Bourgueil, half that of Chinon.

Some commentators have claimed greater depth and concentration for the wines of St-Nicolas compared to its neighbour's; others suggest the opposite. In reality they are indistinguishable: a St-Nicolas

Beautifully tended vines in Bourgueil, the rival of Chinon in producing the finest red wines of the Loire. This is the Domaine du Grand Clos.

grown on sandy soil will more closely resemble a similarly located Bourgueil than another St-Nicolas of gravel or tufa provenance. The two appellations share identical regulations, though previously the maximum yield for St-Nicolas was 5 hectolitres per hectare lower at 35 hectolitres per hectare. Since 1982 they have both been 45 hectolitres per hectare.

St-Nicolas lies to the west of Bourgueil and is home to a number of distinguished growers, including several from the extended Jamet family. Claude and Thierry Amirault make excellent wine in a lighter style at their Clos des Quarterons but the best wines of St-Nicolas usually come from Joel and Clarisse Taluau. Taluau is one of those producers who never stops learning, regularly tasting his own produce and that of his neighbours to try to improve his wine. He realized, for example, that the area's traditional chestnut barrels were giving a harsh aftertaste to the wine, so he switched over to oak after the 1976 vintage and has clearly reaped the benefits.

Pierre Jacques Druet, taking time off to explain his different cuvées of Bourgueil.

TOURAINE – LEADING GROWERS		
Appellation	**Producer**	**Village**
Touraine	Girault-Artois Château de l'Aulée Philippe Brossillon Confrérie des Vignerons Gaston Pavy Domaine du Salvard	Mesland Azay-le-Rideau Mesland Oisly et Thésée Azay-le-Rideau Cheverny
Vouvray	Daniel Allias Frédérick Bourillon Dorléans Marc Brédif *André & Philippe Foreau Benoit Gautier *Gaston Huet Daniel Jarry Prince Philippe Poniatowski	Vouvray Rochecorbon Rochecorbon Vouvray Parçay-Meslay Vouvray Vouvray Vouvray
Montlouis	Berger Frères G. Délétang D. Moyer Gilles Verley	St-Martin-le-Beau St-Martin-le-Beau Montlouis St-Martin-le-Beau
Chinon	Bernard Baudry Jean Baudry Couly-Dutheil *Charles Joguet Pierre Manzagol Jean-François Olek Olga Raffault Domaine du Raifault	Cravant-les-Coteaux Cravant-les-Coteaux Chinon Sazilly Ligré Cravant-les-Coteaux Beaumont-en-Véron Savigny-en-Véron
Bourgueil and St-Nicolas	*Pierre-Jacques Druet Lamé-Delille-Boucard Paul Maître & R. Viémont Joël et Clarisse Taluau	Benais Ingrandes-de-Touraine Benais St-Nicolas
*Outstanding producers		

ANJOU-SAUMUR

The next great district of the Loire stretches from west of Angers to east of Saumur. In 1152 Henry Plantagenet, Count of Anjou, married Eleanor of Aquitaine, uniting the majority of western France under his strong leadership and the Angevin line. Two years later he acceded to the English throne as well.

Nowadays people are more concerned with the wine of Anjou than its history. It is a country widely known for its simple rosé, yet most highly praised for its glorious sweet white wines.

APPELLATIONS OF ANJOU-SAUMUR	
Anjou	Coteaux de l'Aubance
Anjou villages	Savennières
Anjou Coteaux de la Loire	Coulée de Serrant
Rosé d'Anjou	La Roche aux Moines
Cabernet d'Anjou	Saumur
Coteaux du Layon	Coteaux de Saumur
Coteaux du Layon-Chaume	Saumur-Champigny
Quarts de Chaume	Vins du Thouarsais VDQS
Bonnezeaux	

Anjou (Generic Appellations)

Vast quantities of cheap Rosé d'Anjou are exported, as this wine has created a significant market amongst inexperienced wine-drinkers. Light and slightly sweet, it has been a useful introduction to many thousands who now drink more interesting wines.

By law Rosé d'Anjou may be grown from Cabernet Franc, Cabernet Sauvignon, Pineau D'Aunis, Gamay, Cot or Groslot. In practice the latter is responsible for a large proportion. This plentiful red grape lacks the colouring and concentration to produce an acceptable red wine but is well suited to the production of 'easy-drinking' rosé wines. It is usually produced in a medium sweet style.

Finer rosés are produced from Cabernet Franc or Sauvignon under the AC Cabernet d'Anjou, requiring a lower yield and a higher minimum alcohol level. The class of the Cabernet grape is also evident in these wines, which are more elegant and have an appreciably longer aftertaste. They may be produced dry or medium dry.

Cabernet is also the stalwart grape for Anjou Rouge, liable indeed to be specified as Anjou Rouge de Cépage Cabernet on the label. Unlike red wines from Touraine these have a strong representation of Cabernet Sauvignon as well as Cabernet Franc. The grapes blend together well – the Franc has elegance and gorgeous raspberry flavours, but lacks the backbone which the Sauvignon, on its own too harsh, can provide. Where once these grapes might have been converted to swell the sea of rosé, nowadays red wines are more in fashion.

But there is a problem: a traditional long fermentation of the Cabernet grape, in this northern climate, tends to produce a hard, green style of wine with too much tannin. They may very well be *vins de garde* (wines for keeping), but the region does not have a good enough reputation for its red wines to induce connoisseurs to lay them down.

One solution is to experiment with modern techniques of vinification in order to extract colour and character without the harsh components. Passing nitrogen through closed vats, a form of artificial maceration, has proved quite successful to date. This solution is more readily available to merchants or cooperatives rather than individual growers, who in any case might prefer the traditional style.

Red wines may also be made from Gamay, although not in the Saumur part of the appellation. These wines are styled Anjou Gamay and might be made either by traditional fermentation or by the Beaujolais method of *macération carbonique* (see page 24) – not the same as the nitrogen experiments for the Cabernet. These are wines for drinking young.

Traditionally Anjou Blanc would have been made purely from Chenin Blanc but the appellation allows for up to 20 per cent of either Chardonnay or Sauvignon Blanc to be included. The former adds a slightly different dimension to the body of the wine; the latter adds pungency to the bouquet. One can be misled, though, because fermentation at low temperatures can give a Sauvignon-style nose to a young wine which might be 100 per cent Chenin.

If the wines are dry they lack the charm to be of interest outside the region – and then they require a hot day to make their acidity refreshing rather than destructive. The medium dry *demi-sec* version is better balanced for regular consumption, allowing the mouth longer to appreciate the elegance of well-made

Chenin before the acidity takes over. If conditions are suitable a sweeter *moelleux* style is also possible.

Anjou Blanc is not a famous appellation but it has one celebrated producer, the Touchais family with its trademark Moulin Touchais. An astonishing cellar with almost unbelievable stocks of old vintages is regularly 'discovered' by professionals or journalists from one country or another. M. Touchais is able to market commercial quantities of mature sweet wines, sometimes blessed by the noble rot discussed below, at very attractive prices, since the wines only have the right to the appellation Anjou Blanc.

Regulations also exist for Anjou Mousseux but this is rarely made.

The latest appellation in the Loire valley was created in October 1987: Anjou Villages. Its purpose is to strengthen the image of the Cabernet based red wines of the region, underpinning the resurgence they have been enjoying at the expense of rosé wines.

Forty six of the many communes entitled to the straightforward AC Anjou may now promote their red wines, made from Cabernet Franc or Cabernet Sauvignon, to Anjou Villages. The area involved is the heartland of great Chenin Blanc wines, from Savennières through Coteaux du Layon and Coteaux de l'Aubance to Bonnezeaux and beyond. It stretches from Ingrandes and Bouchemaine on the north bank of the Loire as far as Bouille-Loretz in the south.

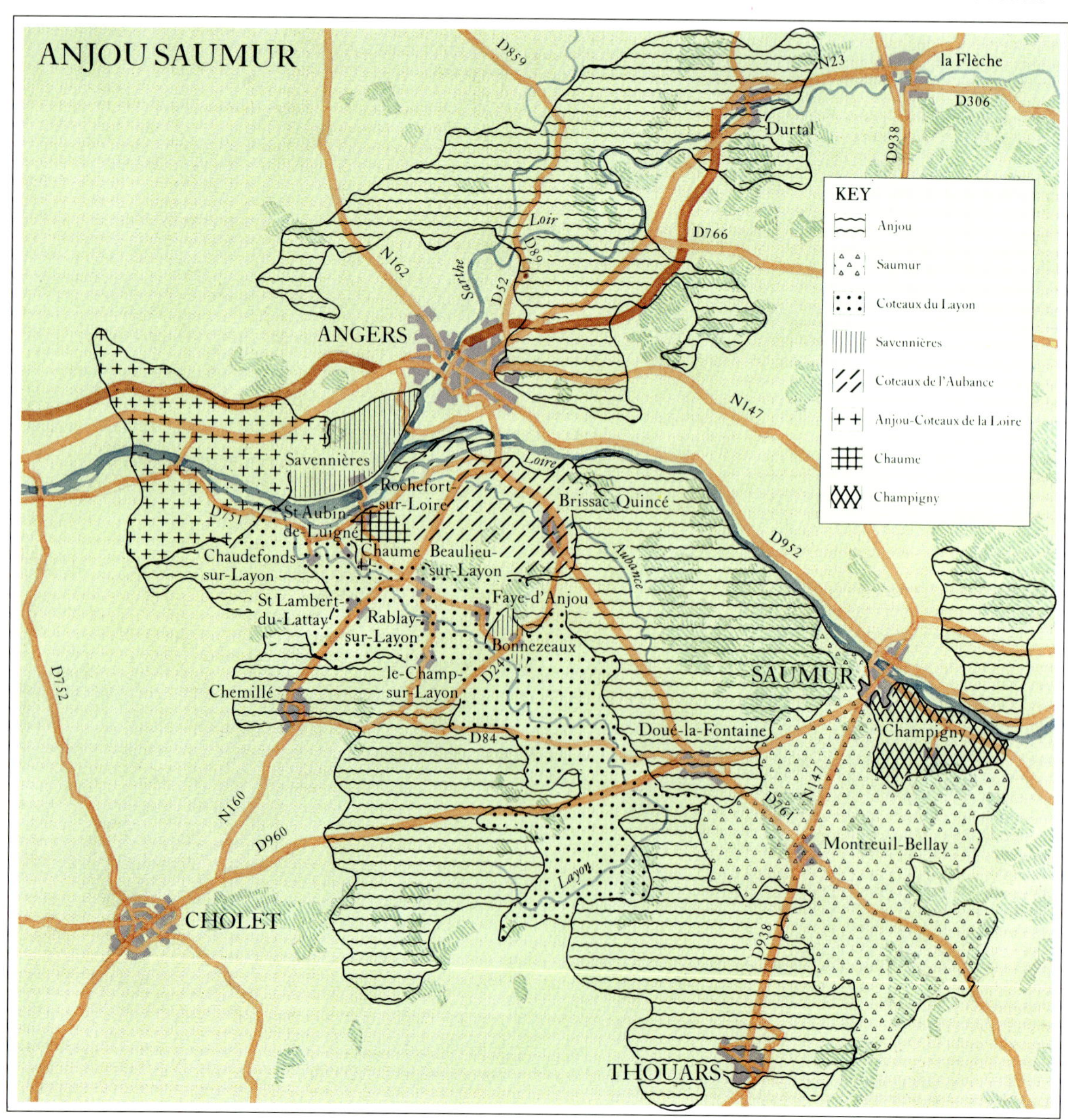

Anjou Coteaux de la Loire

This rare appellation is available for Chenin Blanc wines similar in style to Coteaux du Layon or Coteaux de l'Aubance (described on page 66). It covers a number of communes mostly north of the Loire surrounding the better-known appellation of Savennières.

Saumur

Saumur has a character of its own, independent of Anjou with which it is administratively combined. The town itself, with its gleaming cavalry school, makes a more impressive spectacle than Angers which is influenced by slate rather than stone. The chalk cliffs on the south bank of the Loire west of Saumur have been used to provide housing since prehistoric times.

Several of the same basic appellations apply to Saumur as Anjou, although this is not rosé country. Reds are made from the Cabernets, with Pineau d'Aunis also permitted; whites are from Chenin Blanc, with Chardonnay and Sauvignon allowed up to 20 per cent – exactly as for Anjou. There is also an AC called Coteaux de Saumur for semi-sweet wines to be made solely from Chenin Blanc; the conditions for this are very similar to Anjou Coteaux de la Loire.

The main difference between Saumur and the rest of Anjou is that this is a notable centre for sparkling wines, benefiting from the abundance of chalk in the soil. A number of major companies specializing in the production of sparkling wines are based here, including Gratien & Meyer, a firm which reverses the trend of Champenois houses owning vineyards in the Loire – it owns Champagne Alfred Gratien.

More typically, amongst sparkling Loire producers, Langlois-Chateau is owned by Bollinger, while Taittinger controls Bouvet-Ladubay (Saumur) and Monmousseau (Montrichard, Touraine). Other principal firms making Saumur Mousseux are the interconnected Rémy Pannier and Ackerman-Laurence and Les Caves de la Loire based at Brissac-Quincé.

Saumur Mousseux can be made from almost all of the grape varieties found in the Loire but Chardonnay and Sauvignon are restricted to a maximum of 20 per cent between them and red grapes may not exceed 60 per cent of the blend – except of course in the rosé version.

Though usage of the phrase *méthode champenoise* will be illegal, these wines are indeed made by the same method as champagne. The claim that a good Saumur Mousseux is the equal of many cheap champagnes is often made but is meaningless, since it involves comparing the best of one region with the worst of another, from different grape varieties, offering dissimilar flavours.

Saumur-Champigny

The chalk soil of Saumur is not a friend of Gamay but of Cabernet, especially Cabernet Franc. A wide appellation exists for Saumur Rouge but the best vineyards lie within the more closely delimited area of Saumur-Champigny to the east of the town. This appellation is very much *à la mode* at the moment, the latest Loire wine to be 'discovered' in Paris.

Cabernet Franc produces a lighter wine here than in the Touraine vineyards of Bourgueil and Chinon, but Saumur-Champigny can be charming none the less. A considerable proportion of production is in the hands of the capable cooperative of St-Cyr-en-Bourg but a few individual growers stand out, such as the brothers Dubois, also at St-Cyr, and Paul Filliatreau at Chaintré. Many growers throughout France are keen to stress the age of their vines by marking *vieilles vignes* on the label. As well as doing this for his best *cuvée*, which needs bottle age, M. Filliatreau equally makes a virtue of his *jeunes vignes* wine that supplies the needs of the restaurant trade which requires a suppler style for immediate consumption.

Château du Breuil, welcoming visitors to try their wines, is an important estate in Coteaux du Layon.

Coteaux du Layon

Under the best conditions Chenin Blanc can fulfil its outstanding potential and produce sublimely nuanced sweet wines capable of almost indefinite ageing. On the banks of the River Layon the right combination of sunshine, slopes and soil is found.

This close to the Atlantic the growing season is happily long, with balmy autumns extending the warm weather throughout October. Vineyards on the steep slopes on the north bank of the Layon benefit from maximum exposure to the sun, which is also reflected off the slaty soil of the best vineyards.

With the Layon at their feet and the Loire not far distant, the vines are also subject to greater humidity than elsewhere, a vital factor in the production of great sweet wines. On the ripening grapes a beneficial rot, *pourriture noble*, will form in humid conditions. This concentrates the vital parts of the grape, the sugar and acidity, while imparting an extra flavour of its own. The truly great years, such as 1947 and 1959, are well endowed with this noble rot.

Layon wines require serious commitment on the part of the grower to ensure the quality is suitable. Whereas Anjou Blanc need only achieve 9.5° natural alcohol from a higher yield, Coteaux du Layon must have a potential alcohol, taking into account unconverted sugar, of 12° from a maximum yield of 30 hectolitres per hectare.

The best vineyards within the Coteaux du Layon come from certain favoured villages which have the right to add their names to the appellation. Six of these – Beaulieu, Faye-d'Anjou, Rablay, Rochefort-sur-Loire, St-Aubin-de-Luigné and St-Lambert-du-Lattay – are required to obtain an extra degree of natural alcohol to qualify. A wonderful opportunity to taste a classic mature example of such a wine came recently with the sale of Maison Prunier's cellar, including some 1928 Anjou-Rablay (AC Coteaux du Layon dates from 1950).

More recent vintages of Coteaux du Layon can be enjoyed from winemakers such as Philippe Leblanc, a passionate supporter of wines from Faye, or M. Ravoin-Cesbron whose 1971, fully mature now as a Bonnezeaux would not be, makes a marvellous mouthful, its flavours lingering on the palate.

The seventh village, Chaume, is further distinguished by being restricted to a yield of only 25 hectolitres per hectare, though conscientious growers such as Michel Doucet at Château de la Guimonière frequently fail to reach even this low figure. To make fine wines of this sort it is necessary to pick the grapes only when they are ripe and preferably when affected

A peaceful scene in provincial France: this is Rochefort-sur-Loire, the northernmost of the Coteaux du Layon communes.

Château de la Guimonière still possesses stocks of fabulous older vintages. Here is Michel Doucet about to sample a young version of his Coteaux du Layon Chaume.

by the noble rot if the vintage is generous in that respect. This means sending the pickers more than once through the vineyards and abandoning a fair share to the birds.

The wines of Château de la Guimonière show the difference between a regular Coteaux du Layon and a Chaume. Impressive and inexpensive though the former may be, the extra few francs for the Coteaux du Layon-Chaume is easily repaid by a marked increase in concentration and length. As Madame Doucet's cellar shows, these wines can last for many decades.

Quarts de Chaume

Marvellous though a Coteaux du Layon-Chaume may be, it has to take second place to a wine from the tiny appellation of Quarts de Chaume. The law stipulates Chenin Blanc, 13° minimum potential alcohol and a maximum yield of 22 hectolitres per hectare (the lowest in all the Loire) but those bare facts suggest nothing of the majesty of this wine.

Steep, well-protected slopes produce a microclimate of greater warmth for the production of wines of deeper lusciousness. Even when young these wines indicate the glory they will achieve when mature, many years ahead. They can be appreciated at any age, except perhaps between three and 10 years when sulky adolescence robs the wine of its charms.

Would that these wines were more plentiful, but producers of Quarts de Chaume remain in single figures. Amongst the best known is Jean Baumard, who also produces a fine Coteaux du Layon, Clos Ste-Catherine. Jacques Lalanne and Pascal Laffourcade have rather larger holdings of Quarts de Chaume at Château de Belle Rive and Château de l'Echardière respectively.

Bonnezeaux

The other exceptional *cru* of the Coteaux du Layon district, this one a little larger, is Bonnezeaux, named after a tiny hamlet consisting of a handful of houses and some ruined windmills a kilometre or two from the village of Thouarcé. The same superlatives apply to these wines as to Quarts de Chaume.

Château de Fesles is the exceptional estate in Bonnezeaux. The late Jean Boivin, who worked a valuable apprenticeship in Sauternes at Château d'Yquem, established the fame of this property, especially with his legendary 1947. So great was this vintage that he vinified the grapes from his various parcels of Bonnezeaux separately: one *cuvée* emerged as a dry wine, the remainder reaching different degrees of luscious-

The decayed wooden windmills of Anjou give an air of timeless tranquillity. This is one of several examples near Bonnezeaux.

ness. All are alive today, fabulous to taste, and vary from a translucent amber to a vigorous mahogany for the sweetest, richest *cuvée* of all.

Recently Jacques Boivin, Jean's son, has once again decided to make a separate *cuvée* from his best parcel of vines, known as La Chapelle. The 1985 La Chapelle promises to be truly exceptional.

So majestic are these wines – though never cloying, thanks to the saving grace of Chenin's acidity – that they are best drunk on their own. Many exciting matches with food challenge that idea: can you imagine a bottle of Bonnezeaux of an extremely fine vintage served alongside *foie gras* marinated in the same wine!

Coteaux de l'Aubance

Further to the east, on the banks of the Aubance (more a stream than a river), lies another small and rarely seen appellation. Coteaux de l'Aubance wines are of a similar style and quality to Coteaux du Layon, obeying the same regulations. They do not achieve the greatness of a Quarts de Chaume or Bonnezeaux, nor indeed the price.

The difference in financial reward for a Coteaux de l'Aubance as opposed to an Anjou Rouge grown in the same area is inadequate given the greater costs and the severe restrictions involved, so, therefore, comparatively little wine is made here from Chenin Blanc.

The Joly family have the best sites in Savennières: Coulée de Serrant, as a monopoly, and La Roche aux Moines whose Château is pictured here.

SAVENNIÈRES

Savennières is perhaps the most extraordinary of the great Anjou wines. Made purely from Chenin Blanc, to specifications of low yield and high natural alcohol, it is nevertheless a dry wine.

The appellation is located on the north bank of the Loire, more or less opposite the mouth of the River Layon. Its particularity is in the soil of slate and clay, based on volcanic tufa. Once sweet and semi-sweet wines were made here but now only Château d'Epiré makes a *demi-sec* as well as the more typical dry wine.

These are not beginners' wines, though at first sniff they can be enchanting. A well-made, not over-sulphured example will have a hauntingly fragrant bouquet, a constantly evolving mixture of flowers and fruits, promising great riches in the mouth, indeed suggesting a honeyed sweetness to follow. This does not come, for the wine is nearly bone-dry, austere and marked by the Chenin's ever-present acidity. The fruit is concentrated, the length impressive, but only in the warmer, suppler years does the taste uphold the promise of the bouquet. This is a severe wine which cannot support mediocrity.

As with the region's fine sweet wines, Savennières will be fermented and brought up in barrel for bottling from Easter onwards. One of the most fascinating properties to visit is Château d'Epiré because the barrels are stored in the vaults of the old church in the village of Epiré, bottled stocks being kept upstairs. Also based in Epiré is Yves Soulez who now produces several different wines from Savennières: his own Château de Chamboureau, along with the Domaine de la Bizolière and the Clos du Papillon.

Yves Soulez also has a share in one of the two special vineyards of Savennières, La Roche aux Moines. This and Coulée de Serrant are the equivalent of Grand Cru vineyards, benefiting from steeper slopes and better exposure to the sun than the rest of the appellation. These wines have significantly greater body than a regular Savennières, which enables them to support their acidity better.

The pearl above all is Coulée de Serrant, a 7-hectare vineyard owned solely by Madame Joly, who lives in the impressive converted monastery of the same name as the vineyard. To taste her Roche aux Moines and Coulée de Serrant side by side shows the potential greatness of the latter – still dry but so supple as to be enticingly rich. This wine will certainly last 10 years, often 20 or more for the better vintages – but not many can afford the price now asked.

VINS DU THOUARSAIS

A small VDQS district exists to the south of the main body of Anjou wines, around the town of Thouars in the Deux-Sèvres department. Wines of all three colours are made: Chenin Blanc with up to 20 per cent Chardonnay for the whites, and Cabernet or Gamay for red and rosé.

ANJOU-SAUMUR – LEADING GROWERS

Appellation	Producer	Village
Coteaux du Layon	Jean Baumard Michel Doucet Pierre Yves Tijou	Clos Ste-Catherine Château de la Guimonière Domaine de la Soucherie
Quarts de Chaume	Jean Baumard P. Laffourcade Jacques Lalanne	 Château de l'Echardière Château de Belle Rive
Bonnezeaux	*Jacques Boivin Vincent & Denis Goizil René Renou	Château de Fesles Domaine du Petit Val
Savennières	Mme Bizard-Litzow Mme Jessey Mme Joly Yves Soulez	Château d'Epiré Coulée de Serrant Château de Chamboureau
Saumur	M. & J.-C. Dubois Domaine Filliatreau Vatan Père & Fils Gratien & Meyer Langlois-Chateau	Saumur-Champigny Saumur-Champigny Saumur-Champigny Saumur Mousseux Saumur Mousseux

*Outstanding producers

PAYS NANTAIS

The spirit of the Val de Loire gives way in the Pays Nantais to the influence of the Atlantic here on the marches of Brittany. Though Nantes itself may be ugly and industrial, the surrounding countryside remains as attractive as anywhere along the great river. The vine is prolific, offering a sea of Muscadet of varying qualities and a number of more local wines of all colours. There are no exceptional bottles here but plenty to give pleasure.

APPELLATIONS OF PAYS NANTAIS	
Muscadet	Muscadet de Sèvre-et-Maine
Muscadet des Coteaux de la Loire	Coteaux d'Ancenis VDQS
	Gros Plant VDQS

Muscadet

Muscadet is one of the great success stories of the post-war years. It is established as the foremost white quaffing wine of France, half the price of Sancerre or Pouilly Fumé and much more widely produced. Nearly 100 million bottles of all categories of Muscadet were produced in 1986, 55 per cent being consumed in France and just under a quarter being exported to Britain. Yet scandals and a sea of inferior, cheap wine have dented Muscadet's reputation recently, though these problems should not obscure the quality achieved by more dedicated producers.

The name Muscadet, the 'little musky one', has come to denote the Melon de Bourgogne, a grape imported from eastern France in small quantities in the 17th century and more substantially after the unprecedented freeze of 1709-10. Now this vine sprawls over a substantial portion of the Loire Atlantique department, covering 9,900 hectares in all. Some of this carries the simple Muscadet appellation; another part is designated as Muscadet des Coteaux de la Loire but the lion's share is from the Sèvre-et-Maine appellation.

The catchment area for Muscadet stretches from St-Père-en-Retz and Pornic (on the coast) in the west to Montrevault and Montfaucon in the east, Nantes to the north and Legé and Montaigu by the southern boundary. Many communes come within these bounds but only a handful have more than a few hectares under vine. The most prolific are Tillières, near Montfaucon, the imposingly named St-Philibert-de-Grand-Lieu and La Chapelle-Basse-Mer.

Some good wines are doubtless made for local consumption but it is hard to enthuse about most examples bottled for the mass market. These can so often be dull, over-sulphured and not worth their admittedly low price. If they did not have appellation status they would struggle to find a market.

Muscadet des Coteaux de la Loire

Not much is seen of this smallish appellation lying east of Nantes on both banks of the River Loire. Its catchment area is wide, stretching beyond Ancenis, but other types of farming are more prevalent than vines. In all, the Coteaux de la Loire produces little more than 5 per cent of all Muscadet.

The wines tend to be a touch drier than Sèvre-et-Maine Muscadets, with slightly greater longevity. Even within the Coteaux de la Loire there are variations according to soil. Most vines are on clay and schist but other soils intrude: flint is common at St-Herblon, yielding clean austere wines.

Best-known grower in this region, indeed the only one whose wines appear regularly outside France, is Jacques Guindon at St-Géréon on the outskirts of Ancenis. Jacques and his son Pierre are the third and fourth generations of Guindons here, an ancestor having made the great trek from just across the river at the end of last century.

Muscadet de Sèvre-et-Maine

For many, this appellation is synonymous with Muscadet. Indeed a Muscadet Grand Cru de Sèvre-et-Maine classification was established ten years before *appellation contrôlée* came to the region in 1936. Sèvre-et-Maine now covers more than 80 per cent of production, including some of the best examples but also a fair share of the horrors.

Wines made from Muscadet are not vibrant with flavour. It is a neutral grape, not too acidic, dry and light. It is difficult to spot in a blind tasting, the flavour not recalling any specific fruit to jog the memory. Muscadet must always be a light wine because, unique amongst appellation regulations, a maximum alcohol level of 12° is specified – though it may be revised in exceptional years.

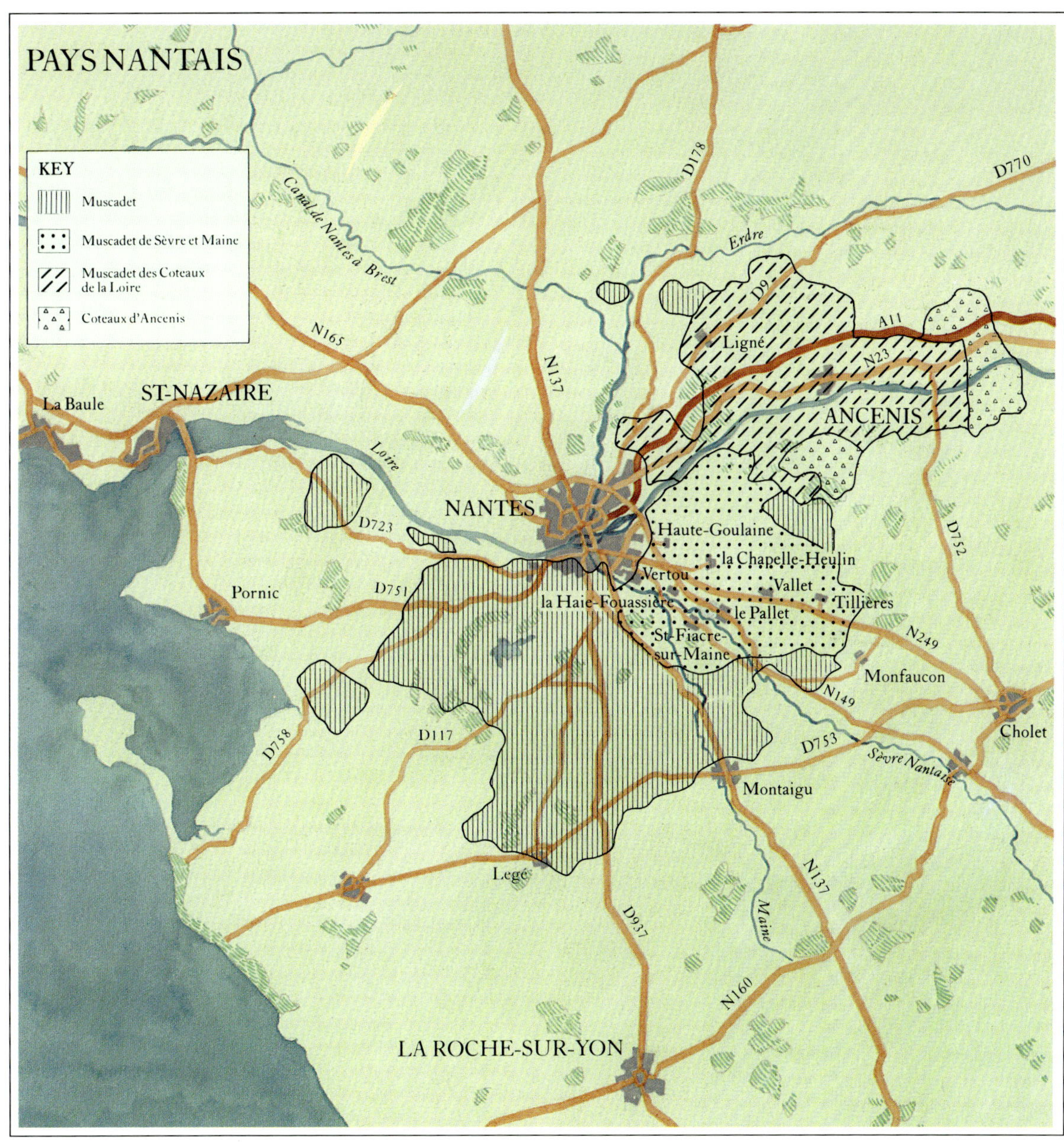

The simpler wines can offer no more than an agreeable neutrality, but the mass-produced examples are too often spoiled by overdoses of sulphur. Their success in the marketplace is due to the combination of their appellation status and low price – but France can offer better wines more cheaply, though they may only be classified as *vins de pays*.

But plenty of more exciting and cleanly made Muscadets are available. This wine can be one of the great thirst-quenchers, a gulping wine to be drunk at any hour on its own or to accompany Atlantic coast seafood at lunch or dinner.

Many of the better Muscadets will have been bottled *sur lie*. The principle is that the wine benefits from prolonged contact with the dead yeast cells which have formed a sediment, the lees. The resulting wine should have a richer bouquet, the dead lees adding a yeasty character to the light fruitiness, while a trace of carbon dioxide lends *pétillance* to each bottle, preserving the wine's freshness. There is no shortage of really attractive wines of this sort, from individual domaines or larger concerns, and, for an extra 5 francs at the cellar door, these are clearly the wines to buy.

The attractive village of Loroux-Bottereau which is a major centre for production of Muscadet.

Of course it would be easy enough to label a bottle of Muscadet *sur lie* and not to bother with the genuine process and there are suspicions that this sometimes happens. As a preventative measure the regulations for *sur lie* bottling stipulate that the grower must bottle his wine directly from the lees before the end of June following the vintage. If the wine is to be bottled by a *négociant* it must be moved to his premises before the end of March. Said premises have to be within the AC Muscadet district, so merchants upriver cannot genuinely bottle Muscadet *sur lie* at their own headquarters.

Muscadet is for drinking young but the better wines from good vintages will certainly keep, even beyond a decade. The youthful fruit fades to be replaced by a plumper, mellowed grace. This is especially true of Muscadet from those few growers who still make their wine in wooden barrels. Notable amongst these are the Château du Cléray, the Château de la Noë, Joseph Hallereau's Clos des Hautes Bretonnières and the Chéreau-Carré family.

Muscadet de Sèvre-et-Maine covers in whole or in part 23 communes, by no means all of which lie between the two named rivers. (The importance of such a location is heavily stressed by those who own vines there; unaccountably it is considered insignificant by those who do not!)

The visitor might not discern significant geographical differences across the region but the locals can point to variations in style from one village to the next. Despite the nearby industrial presence of Nantes this is really an area of hamlets, villages and one or two small towns. Winding lanes and the little streams which feed the Loire, Sèvre and Maine rivers form a latticework frequently interrupted by the spires of scores of village churches. This is rural not suburban France.

Close to the confluence of the Sèvre and the Maine lies the village of St-Fiacre. Just across the Sèvre is La Haie-Fouassière, rather larger. These two provide the focal point for some of the very best Muscadet. Indeed, driving through the drab flatter parts of the region makes a sharp contrast to this particular corner where the slopes are steeper and the vines better tended. The view from Jean Dabin's Gras Mouton vineyard impresses in every direction – nothing but vines and distant church spires.

A good Muscadet from St-Fiacre should be the most charming of the whole region: elegant, subtly perfumed and softly pleasing to the palate, yet with a flinty edge derived from the soil. The Chéreau-Carrés between them are lucky enough to own six properties here, including the Moulin de la Gravelle and the Château de Chasseloir. Another, Château du Coing de St-Fiacre, is situated right at the confluence of the two rivers. All the Chéreau-Carré wines from their own properties (they are also *négociants*) are produced in wood, while their latest idea is a wine from Château de Chasseloir made entirely in new barrels. It ought not to work, and certainly the wine does not taste like a typical Muscadet, but the fruit survives the drying-out effects of new oak successfully.

Rival to St-Fiacre is the small market town of Vallet, further to the east and well outside the immediate influence of the two rivers. Here the soil is cooler and heavier, being predominantly of clay, and its wines take on a different style. They are firmer in structure, slower to open out and longer-lasting. In a region where bottling may take place as early as January or February, typical Vallet wines are not usually ready until Easter.

Other villages of note are Mouzillon, just south of Vallet, Le Pallet, nearer to the River Sèvre, and La Chapelle-Heulin, also to the west. The vineyard area also stretches to the north to take in Haute-Goulaine, where the eleventh Marquis de Goulaine runs an important operation. The family have been there for over a thousand years, hence the name of their top wine, Cuvée du Millénaire.

Commerce in the Pays Nantais is dominated by merchants and individual growers, cooperatives taking a back seat. Several of the more important producers have strong ideas about the future development of Muscadet. Should there be some form of superior appellation, a Muscadet-Villages for example, with leading communes such as those discussed above entitled to stress their name on the label? Three well-known producers have each taken similar but subtly different paths in promoting the beloved wines of their region.

Louis Métaireau has a special reputation. He leads a small association of growers who rigorously taste each *cuvée* of the new season's production before choosing different wines with various qualities to bear the Métaireau name. There is the Domaine du Grand Mouton, jointly owned; the Coupe Louis Métaireau, which is destined specifically for the restaurant trade; and the apogee, Cuvée 1, which sells for an even greater premium than the others. Absolute dedication and commitment to quality is worth paying for. Métaireau's son-in-law, Jean-François Guilbaud, supports the same ideal by selecting superior *cuvées* and bottling them for the individual grower.

Advances in technology may change the equipment in the cellars but chez Gallais the ancient wooden press still has its uses.

The wines of the Pays Nantais, especially searingly dry Gros Plant, are excellent with oysters.

Another 'super-cuvée' is Le Master de Donatien. An international panel, including British Masters of Wine, meets over a weekend to sift through countless *cuvées* in order to achieve the finest blend the firm of Donatien-Bahuaud can muster. Quality and assertive marketing are not mutually exclusive here as they so often seem to be.

The firm of Sauvion & Fils has also devised a way of promoting the region in general at the same time as ensuring top-quality wines in their portfolio. Their idea is Les Découvertes de Sauvion, a range of 10 to 15 wines which come from individual domaines but are selected and bottled by themselves. The selection is made afresh each year, so one producer might feature regularly year after year but another only on his best form. The grower will receive a significant premium for his wine if it is chosen – a premium which could not be matched if he were tied to a regular contract.

Aside from these and other celebrated producers there is a host of top-quality growers, each with his or her own domaine or château. Most have typical Breton names, similar-sounding and often confusing. For example, there is no connection between the Château de l'Oiselinière at Gorges, near Clisson, and M. Chéreau's Château de l'Oiselinière de la Ramée at St-Fiacre.

Gros Plant du Pays Nantais

The region's second wine is an acquired taste whose greatest merit is the match it makes with oysters freshly hauled off the Atlantic beds. Bitingly green, it matches the saltiness and cuts across the 'plumpness' of a plateful of them.

The Dutch were responsible for establishing Gros Plant at the mouth of the Loire. They brought the Folle Blanche, producer of thin white wines in Cognac country north, and it rapidly became the most widely planted vine in the Pays Nantais. It has since been superseded by Muscadet and accounts for under a quarter of the region's vineyard area.

Gros Plant, as the grape has come to be known, qualifies for VDQS status and sells in bulk for just over half the average price of Muscadet. It may be produced and sold *sur lie*, subject to exactly the same controls as Muscadet, but is less often found in this form. Gros Plant already possesses a sufficiently assertive character and does not need such a variation.

Well made, from a warmer year, and drunk in the region, Gros Plant can provide an agreeable glass of wine. It is difficult to justify selecting it elsewhere or under less favourable conditions, when the mouth undeniably puckers.

Coteaux d'Ancenis

On both banks of the Loire, on either side of Ancenis, quite a variety of different grapes are grown. Muscadet comes under the appellation Coteaux de la Loire; the remainder are VDQS Coteaux d'Ancenis. Four varieties are possible – Cabernet, Gamay, Chenin Blanc and Pinot Gris – and the relevant one must be stipulated on the label.

Most production is red or rosé from Gamay, giving light, agreeable fruity wines, attractive locally but of no wider significance. Most of the Gamay vines are of the classic Beaujolais type but a few hybrids remain. Of slightly more interest, though again really for local consumption, is the Cabernet wine which may come from either variety, Sauvignon or Franc. Good examples can be very powerful, needing several years' ageing.

Some austere white wines are made from Chenin Blanc (Pineau de la Loire) but the local excitement comes from the Pinot Gris (Pinot Beurot), here known as Malvoisie. Jacques Guindon owns 2 of the 3½ hectares still planted with Malvoisie, from which he makes a honeyed, spicy *demi-sec* wine, delicious young but capable of ageing. After 35 years a Malvoisie 1953 still had a great deal to offer – just lightly maderized but with a rich flavour underneath.

Joseph Hallereau holds forth in front of his barrels. These are now a rare sight in the Pays Nantais although one or two growers are experimenting with new wood.

PAYS NANTAIS – LEADING GROWERS		
Producer	**Estate**	**Village**
Bossis	Château de la Cantrie	St-Fiacre
Chéreau-Carré	Château de Chasseloir	St-Fiacre
	Domaine du Bois Bruley	St-Fiacre
	Grand Fief du Cormeraie	St-Fiacre
Jean Dabin	Domaine de Gras Mouton	St-Fiacre
Jacques Guindon	Domaine Guindon	Ancenis
Joseph Hallereau	Clos des Hautes Bretonnières	Vallet
Comte Malestroit	Château de la Noë	Vallet
Louis Métaireau	Domaine du Grand Mouton	St-Fiacre
Sauvion & Fils	Château du Cléray	Vallet
	Les Découvertes de Sauvion	

VIN DE PAYS AND OUTLYING VINEYARDS

Mostly it is Appellation Controlée wines which thrive on the export markets but they do not have a monopoly of pleasant drinking. Visit the Loire and you may enjoy many cheerful carafes of Vins de Pays. Upstream, as the Loire tumbles through the Massif Central, are pockets of vineyards supplying the local restaurants and rural population.

Vins de Pays

In the years before the phylloxera bug much of France was covered in vines. Since then the vine has been concentrated in the most receptive areas but plenty of rural pockets still exist. These are classified as Vins de Table but usually fall within the category of Vins de Pays. These are grouped in three styles: according to local descriptions, by department, or belonging to a major region.

The all-encompassing title of the wines of the Loire is Vin de Pays du Jardin de la France, covering ten departments. These ten, plus Sarthe and Nièvre, may also use the departmental title but this is usually less popular for marketing reasons than Jardin de la France. The only ones seen with any regularity are Loir-et-Cher, Indre-et-Loire and Maine-et-Loire.

The three locally described Vins de Pays (see box) are also rarely seen. There was a fourth, Fiefs Vendéens, which was promoted to VDQS in 1984.

VINS DE PAYS

Vin de Pays du Jardin de la France

Vin de Pays des Coteaux du Cher et de l'Arnon
Vin de Pays des Marches de Bretagne
Vin de Pays de Retz

Vin de Pays de la Nièvre
Vin de Pays du Cher
Vin de Pays de l'Indre
Vin de Pays du Loiret
Vin de Pays de la Sarthe
Vin de Pays du Loir-et-Cher
Vin de Pays de l'Indre-et-Loire
Vin de Pays du Maine-et-Loire
Vin de Pays de la Loire-Atlantique
Vin de Pays de la Vendée
Vin de Pays de la Vienne
Vin de Pays des Deux-Sèvres

In practice, 60 per cent of Loire Vin de Pays comes under the Jardin de la France label, a proportion which will grow. In most instances the wines will be made of a single grape variety as specified on the label. White wines (30 per cent) come mostly from Chenin or Sauvignon with some Arbois, Chardonnay, Pinot Blanc and Pinot Gris wines. Rosé production (20 per cent) is mainly from Grolleau (Groslot) and Pineau d'Aunis, while the principal red varieties are Gamay and the two Cabernets.

Côtes du Forez

Shortly after bypassing the industrial centre of St-Etienne, the Loire flows through the upland plain of the Forez – a name apparently derived from the Roman town of Forum Segusianorum rather than being a corruption of *forêt*. The vineyard area, Côtes du Forez, is planted with Gamay to make a lighter version of Beaujolais – which district is within 100 kilometres as the crow flies.

These are agreeable wines for local consumption – perhaps with one of the excellent cheeses of this part of the Massif Central, such as Fourme d'Ambert.

Côte Roannaise

Flowing on from the Côtes du Forez, the Loire comes to Roanne, the town made gastronomically famous by the brothers Troisgros. The local tipple is similar in style to the previous region: a light red wine made from Gamay. Once again its merit is more as a local carafe wine than as a bottled product to be drunk away from its home.

Côtes d'Auvergne

Switching rivers, we find wines from the Côtes d'Auvergne on the Allier near Clermont-Ferrand. As well as the straightforward appellation which covers the *arrondissements* of Clermont-Ferrand, Riom and Issoire, five more specific appellations are detailed. Boudes, Chanturgue, Châteaugay, Corent and Madargues may each add their name as a suffix to Côtes d'Auvergne.

Red and rosé wines are made from Gamay and Pinot Noir; Chardonnay provides the white wines. The Gamay is the most widely planted, making successful reds for local consumption at Chanturgue.

St-Pourçain

The Allier has a small tributary, the Sioule, on which stands the little market town of St-Pourçain. Recognizing that the appellation's full title was too much of a mouthful, the authorities have now removed the river from the original name of the town St-Pourçain-sur-Sioule.

Unlike the wines so far described in this section, St-Pourçain has attracted sufficient interest outside the area for bottles to be exported. The red wines may be made from Gamay or Pinot Noir; the whites come from an intriguing hotch-potch of varieties local and imported. Tressallier may compose up to half the blend, St-Pierre Doré (which sounds more like a fish) up to 10 per cent, while there is no specified limit to the proportions of Sauvignon, Chardonnay or Aligoté.

To find Aligoté in this part of France is a surprise, as it also is to discover that Tressallier is a synonym for Sacy, the minor white grape of the Yonne. The implication is of cross-pollination with the Chablis district. After this ampelographical treat, it is a shame to report that most of the white wines err on the side of tartness.

Châteaumeillant

Moving further west, on the borders of the departments of Cher and Indre, is Châteaumeillant, an appellation covering eight communes. The vineyards are planted with Gamay, Pinot Gris and Pinot Noir.

Vins du Haut Poitou

North and west of Poitiers, in the department of Vienne (but stretching into Deux-Sèvres), lies the vineyard area of Haut Poitou. Once as unknown as the other rural outcrops of the vine, Haut Poitou has been one of the greatest success stories of the 1980s. The credit for this goes to the *cave coopérative* at Neuville-de-Poitou, where common sense, modern installations and an equal flair for production and marketing have produced an international success. Gold medals are regularly won while competitive pricing ensures no shortage of export orders.

The regulations allow for white wines from Sauvignon, Chardonnay, Pinot Blanc and Chenin Blanc (up to 20 per cent). Red and rosé wines may come from Pinot Noir, Gamay, Merlot (we are halfway to St-Emilion at Poitiers), Cot, both Cabernets and Groslot (up to 20 per cent). The cooperative at Neuville markets four main wines: Sauvignon Blanc, Chardonnay, Gamay (red) and a Cabernet Rosé which tastes much better than its virulent cherry colour suggests it will.

Fiefs Vendéens

In 1984 Vin de Pays des Fiefs Vendéens was promoted to VDQS status. Nineteen communes in the department of Vendée are included, being divided into four locations – Mareuil, Brem, Vix and Pissotte – and the relevant name must be specified on the label.

The red and rosé wines must consist of at least 50 per cent Gamay or Pinot Noir (or both) while Cabernet Sauvignon, Cabernet Franc and Negrette may make up the remainder. The less common white wines must be at least 50 per cent Chenin Blanc while Sauvignon and Chardonnay are also allowed. So too is up to 20 per cent of Melon de Bourgogne (Muscadet) for Vix and Pissotte, while Groslot can also be included in white and rosé wines in Brem.

APPELLATIONS OF THE OUTLYING VINEYARDS

Côtes du Forez	Châteaumeillant
Côte Roannaise	Vins du Haut Poitou
Côtes d'Auvergne	Fiefs Vendéens
St-Pourçain	

The appellations listed in the box currently have VDQS status. They all come within the responsibilities of the Comité Régional du Val de Loire, even if most are not conventionally regarded as Loire vineyards. Some names are virtually unknown outside their regions; others, such as Haut-Poitou, have established reputations in their own right.

INDEX

Figures in *italics* refer to captions to illustrations.

ACKNOWLEDGEMENTS

The Publishers would like to thank the following organisations and photographers for their kind permission to reproduce their photographs: Anthony Blake Photographic Library 70-1; Michael Busselle 17, 36-7, 45, 50, 61, 65, 72-3; Patrick Eager 1, 2-3, 8-9, 25, 27, 42, 56-7, 62-3; Robert Harding Picture Library/Alan Carr 55; Image Bank 74; Images Colour Library 15, 38, 48-9; Mary Stow 1988 21, 26, 40, 44, 52, 58, 64, 66, 75.

Editor: Isobel Greenham
Art Editor and Designer: Bob Gordon
Picture Research: Julia Pashley

Map illustrations: Andrew Farmer
Grape illustrations: Nicki Kemball